Credit Union Collaborations

Lessons Learned

Guy A. Messick

Copyright © 2019 Guy A. Messick

All rights reserved.

ISBN: 9781696937900

DEDICATION

This book is dedicated to my colleagues in the credit union industry who have the vision, the drive and the fortitude to form and develop collaborations that will be the foundation of their credit unions' success for years to come. I thank my law partners and family who have tolerated my travel schedule to promote and serve credit union collaborations. I am grateful to the late John Unangst, former president of Franklin Mint Federal Credit Union and Chair of the NACUSO Board, who connected me to the credit union and CUSO world.

CONTENTS

	Forward	i
1	My Background	1
2	The Evolution of Credit Unions and CUSO's	7
3	Introduction to Credit Union Collaborations	19
4	Lessons Learned Over Thirty Years	25
5	Building a CUSO Business Model	41
6	NACUSO	69
7	Profiles of Notable CUSO's	77
	Epilogue	105
	Appendix: Sample Collaboration Policy	107

FORWARD

I have had the pleasure and honor of working with credit unions for over thirty years, helping them plan, form and operate credit union service organizations ("CUSO's"). CUSO's are organizations that credit unions own or co-own that facilitate collaboration solely among credit unions or between credit unions and third parties.

Actually, the pleasure and honor has been working with credit union and CUSO professionals. You cannot find nicer clients. Credit union folks are intelligent and focused on the well-being of the members. They are also a lot of fun. I have made life-long friendships. Credit unions have enabled me to provide for my family and travel across this wonderful country and world.

This book is a career capstone of sorts. I have acquired knowledge and experience that would be helpful to pass on to the next generation of credit union professionals. The lessons learned can also be applied to collaborations of other cooperatives and fraternal organizations as most of the lessons deal with people and how they interact. Through these pages, I am speaking to the management and directors of credit unions and other cooperatives.

My law partner, Brian Lauer, wrote a book entitled *CUSO's*. His book is a comprehensive window into the CUSO world and I commend it to you. This book examines how collaborations are influenced by human behavior, culture and business structure. Why do some collaborations succeed and why do some fail? How should we think about collaborations in a realistic and practical way? What should a credit union's policies be on collaborations? A sample collaboration policy is provided in the Appendix.

I begin the book with a discussion of my background so that the reader will know the experience from which I speak. In order to give context, I discuss how credit unions and the world in which they operate have evolved to include CUSO's. One of the reasons I wanted to write this book is to preserve knowledge of notable CUSO's.

Some have called me the "CUSO Guru." I am not sure how that came into being other than I was the CUSO "guy" before CUSO's were cool and "guru" is an alliteration. The name seemed to appear spontaneously. I cannot take credit (or blame) for it. Now that I am old enough to look like a guru, I have decided to embrace the brand. So, think of me as a guy with a long flowing beard sitting on a rock dispensing ambiguous advice to no one in particular, that people do not fully understand but find profound in some mystical way.

To all my credit union and CUSO colleagues: Be wise grasshoppers, the future of credit unions is in your hands.

CHAPTER 1
MY BACKGROUND

Before Credit Unions
I grew up in Media, Pennsylvania working for my parents in the restaurant business. My entrepreneurial and small business focus comes from being exposed to that world at an early age.

The career plans made in college do not always pan out. I thought I was going to be a foreign service officer, maybe even an ambassador. My college major at Bucknell University was International Relations and I was fairly good at it. I was fascinated by maps. I would spend hours studying maps and learning about the people that lived in far-off places. I was selected to be a teaching assistant in International Relations.

Most people do not know I played college football. I had to quit the team in my sophomore year after a couple of concussions. No big loss for the team. I was of average size and speed in high school and somehow the players got bigger and faster in college.

Instead of heading off to the State Department, I went to law school after Bucknell. Being a lawyer seemed appealing. I especially liked the concept of performing as a trial lawyer in a courtroom. So, I packed up my bags and went off to the University of Miami Law School. I told myself I could still do the international thing. International law and admiralty law sounded cool.

During the three years of law school, I spent time on the criminal side working as an intern in the District Attorney's Office in my hometown of Media, Pennsylvania in the summer and working as a trial intern in the Miami-Dade County Florida Public Defender's Office during my senior year. I tried criminal cases in Florida with mixed success.

At Miami, I participated on the school's International Moot Court Team. Not much of a surprise there. But surprisingly, we won the best legal brief in the nation and I won the best oralist in the Southern Regional despite my Yankee accent. So, with that on my resume plus being the Chief Justice of the Honor Council (think a long black robe over cut-off shorts), I was able to land a federal judicial clerkship in Seattle.

I loved Seattle and took the bar exam in Washington State. I still maintain my license in Washington State as well as in Pennsylvania. My legal clerkship experience honed my writing skills. I wrote memos and drafts of decisions for U.S. District Judge Morell Sharp, a kind and patient man.

After one year, I decided to return to Media and work full time for the District Attorney's Office as an Assistant District Attorney. I wrote briefs and argued cases before the Pennsylvania Superior Court and Supreme Court. It was heady stuff for a young lawyer.

Next, I joined the largest law firm in Media,

Fronefield & deFuria. I started out doing everything no one else wanted to do. The experience was valuable but my entrepreneurial spirit led me to leave the comfort of a big firm and start my own firm. The name of the firm today is Messick Lauer & Smith. Along the way I became known for municipal law, zoning law, and small business representation. I represented the local chamber of commerce and government economic development agencies. There were a few jury trials too, but my Perry Mason fantasy of the law did not pan out. My opportunities and interest lay elsewhere.

My Path to Credit Unions

In the beginning of my legal career, one of my high school classmates asked me to review documents for the British Petroleum Federal Credit Union. He worked for the refinery and had responsibility for the credit union as part of his job. As a young lawyer you say yes to practically everything. Ignorance of the law is not a barrier to new business. Learning on the job is second nature to a new attorney. I reviewed the credit union's loan documents. In those pre-CFPB days and before the blossoming of the other consumer protection agencies, there were fewer regulatory traps for a novice attorney.

My next connection with credit unions came through my high school girlfriend. She married John Unangst, president of Franklin Mint Federal Credit Union. John was an ex-banker and decorated Vietnam Veteran. When he left the bank and began working at the Credit Union it had three employees, including him. The only office was a big closet that contained three desks next to the Franklin Mint loading dock. Today, the Credit Union has assets of over one billion dollars and twenty-three branch locations.

John needed an inexpensive young lawyer and I fit the bill. I began to learn the regulations and understand credit unions. John was a forward thinker. I helped John form one of the first CUSO's in 1986. The CUSO, State Financial Network, provided mortgage lending and IT services to multiple credit unions. This was radical thinking back in the day. As a CUSO pioneer, John was asked to became a director of the newly formed National Association of Credit Union Service Organizations ("NACUSO") in 1987.

We all know that a credit union folks, by nature, love conferences in nice places. CUSO people are no different. John asked me to go with him to San Diego on his dime to a NACUSO Conference and play golf. My bags were packed before he finished his invitation. NACUSO needed an attorney. John figured he could lure me to NACUSO by sponsoring me to play golf in beautiful places. He was right. I was a push over. My most attractive feature was that I was free. So began my representation of NACUSO in 1987.

Representing NACUSO has been one of the highlights of my professional life. The NACUSO Presidents; Bob Dorsa, Tom Davis, Vic Pantea and Jack Antonini; have each made significant contributions to NACUSO. The NACUSO Admin, Shawna Luna, is a good friend and beloved by the members. A more recent addition to the staff, Denise Wymore, has brought energy and creativity to member communications and recruitment.

The part of our practice that excites me is helping credit unions create and expand CUSO's and other collaborative relationships. How can we structure a relationship between organizations and people that will reward all participants on a personal and professional level? Collaboration is not easy. It is not altruistic. It is finding people with the right values and incentives to work together to achieve a common goal. It is a challenge but when it works, it can provide amazing results.

I like being at the center of the action in the credit

union industry. Our firm, Messick Lauer & Smith, interacts at the crossroads of credit unions, regulators, Congress, entrepreneurs and innovators. We have worked with credit unions and CUSO's in every state. As General Counsel to NACUSO, our firm has helped influence regulations. In 2012 and 2016, I was able to bring the CUSO story overseas to Ireland. I was asked by the University of Cork to teach Irish credit unions about CUSO's.

A highlight of my career is being named one of the three inaugural CUSO Pioneers in America's Credit Union Museum in Manchester, New Hampshire. I share that honor with the late Dave Serlo of PSCU and Sarah Canepa Bang of FSCC and COOP Financial Services; two people I admire.

All of this was made possible by not burning a bridge with my high school girlfriend. There is a lesson there.

CREDIT UNION COLLABORATIONS

CHAPTER 2
THE EVOLUTION OF CREDIT UNIONS AND CUSO'S

The Old Days

Credit unions were disrupters. Ordinary people and small businesses in the United States in the early 20th Century did not have universal access to affordable people-centric financial services. Banks were reluctant to loan to "ordinary people" at competitive rates. They had a monopoly on financial services. Just as the financially underserved people in England and Germany did in the 19th Century, Americans came together and formed credit unions to serve themselves. By pooling their savings in credit unions, people were able to provide loans and deposit services on fair and competitive terms. Credit unions disrupted the status quo and took advantage of a critical need in the marketplace. Credit unions were truly a movement by the people for the people.

For most of the 20th Century consumer financial services were offered on a local scale by community banks and credit unions. People would not travel far for financial services. Financial services competitors were within a short driving distance of each other. The services offered by credit unions were simple and uncomplicated, i.e., savings accounts, checking accounts, and consumer loans.

The people who ran credit unions were often volunteers or low-paid part-time employees. Credit unions were mostly single-sponsored, serving only the employees (and their families) of a single company or parishioners of a church. The technology investment was the cost of an adding machine. The costs of operating financial institutions were low, stable and predictable. There was very little outsourcing of duties. The model was simple. You pay interest on the deposit accounts at X percent and earn interest on the loans at X plus three or four percent. Credit unions were able to live on the net interest margin for most of the 20th Century. We no longer live in a world were credit unions pay dividends of 4% on share accounts and make loans with yields of 8%.

Technology and the Internet

At the end of the 20th Century two things occurred that changed the credit union world forever, the widespread use of technology and the world's adoption of the Internet as a method of commerce. Technology added significant cost factors of people, equipment and software but technology also made the operational processes much more efficient. How much technology helped a credit union often depended on the credit union's size. As the scale of a business increases, the cost of the supporting technology increases at a disproportionately smaller rate so the technology cost per transaction is greatly reduced. The smaller credit unions that cannot afford to keep up with technology costs to remain competitive became less economically viable. The consequences of this lack of scale is one factor driving credit union mergers. However, there are always bigger fish. Even as credit unions merge and grow their scale, the greater scale in the banking industry remains a competitive issue for all credit unions.

In 1969, the number of credit unions in the United States was over 21,000. The technology adoption trend in financial institutions began in the seventies. As of 2019, the number of credit unions has declined by over 70% from the 1969 level and continues to decrease at the rate of about three (3%) percent per year. I anticipate that the adoption of artificial intelligence technology tools will accelerate the chasm between the technology "haves" and "have-nots."

The introduction of the Internet enabled the power of technology to be leveraged worldwide. The near monopoly that financial institutions enjoyed in consumer and business lending, due partially to geographic proximity to customers, is gone forever. The Internet made it more convenient for members to interact with their credit union, but the Internet also made it more convenient for members to interact with hundreds of banks and FinTech competitors. The FinTech's are not equally burdened with corresponding costs of regulatory compliance, physical infrastructure and legacy technology issues. The scale of these Internet competitors enables them to live with razor thin margins earned with loan interest rates that are often more competitive than interest rates offered at credit unions. Each year FinTech companies are taking more and more share of the lending market, especially in the younger demographics.

Non-bank payment competitors have also emerged. Control of payment systems once was a monopoly for financial institutions but that is no longer the case. PayPal, Venmo, the Apple Pay – Goldman Sachs Credit Card, cell phone carriers and other disrupters have positioned themselves to reduce the financial institution industries' share of the payments market each year.

Point of Sale Lending
Beginning in the 1990's, point of sale loans started to

erode credit union lending opportunities. Direct car loan opportunities for credit unions declined as car dealers made more loans at the point of sale. It is hard to imagine now but there was a huge debate among credit unions in the 1990's whether they should sully themselves and get into indirect lending arrangements with car dealers or remain "pure" and continue to have only a direct loan channel. Of course, survival instincts won that debate and indirect auto loans now make up a significant portion of credit union loans. The problem is that the world keeps changing. Local car dealers are now being disrupted as points of sales for cars are now online (e.g., Carvana), leaving both the dealers and their credit union lending partners isolated from some business opportunities. With the requirement that loans can only be made to members, credit unions will find it very difficult to be a lender at points of sale on the Internet which require quick closings.

Changing Service Level Expectations

The bar on what constitutes consumer's expectations of swift, effective and convenient service keeps rising thanks to the FinTech's. Consumers expect a personal loan to be approved and funded before the coffee gets cold. According to Quicken Loan (a/k/a Rocket Mortgage), a mortgage approval can take as little as eight minutes. As time goes by, the consumer expectations are only going to become harder to meet. We have seen the early FinTech competitors providing services with lightning fast turn-around times be disrupted by newer FinTech's that are even faster. This trend is irreversible. If a credit union cannot keep up with the service delivery pace of the FinTech competitors, it will be left in the dust.

The ability to acquire, store, analyze and act on data ties directly into meeting member expectations. Credit unions have an image of themselves that they are close to their members and know their financial needs but that image in most cases is just that, an image. Today, Google and Amazon likely know much more about a credit union's members than the credit union. If a credit union's competitor has the ability to leverage data on a credit union's membership better than the credit union, there is little doubt of the outcome of that competition. Leveraging data enables a credit union to provide product offerings that are relevant and timely to specific members, anticipate loan pay-offs and provide modifications to keep the loans, ask less but more relevant questions in the underwriting process and undercut the competition on loan rates with better data on credit risk.

You remember Kodak, Blockbuster and Borders. Advances in technology and their refusal to change their business model turned them from vibrant companies to business school case studies on the consequences of the failure to adapt to changing market conditions. A credit union is left with no alternative but to develop or buy access to the technology to keep the credit union relevant in the marketplace.

Branches and Mobile Devices

Branches still matter. Members are reassured when they see that their credit union has a branch in their community. It reassures them that they are dealing with a real organization where they can have a face-to-face conversation if they have a problem to solve. There is a growing segment of members who may never go into the branch. Their branch is in their pocket. If a credit union cannot deliver a full suite of services efficiently through mobile devices, the credit union will eventually suffer the same fate as other businesses that have lost to the Internet business model. They will be "Blockbuster-ed" out of business.

Compliance Costs

Credit unions have unsustainable compliance costs

not shared by their FinTech competitors. Credit unions are required to expend costs to fight crime and terrorism (BSA and OFAC) and to add processes and procedures to prevent consumer abuses they did not cause. While the goals of these laws are in the public interest, it is the credit union member that pays for the costs, driving up the price of financial services. The danger is that credit union members will obtain their financial services from providers who do not have to pass along these compliance costs. Excessive compliance cost is cited as one of the principal reasons driving small credit unions to merge.

Sluggish Economy

The growth in the economy is at a slower rate since the 2008 financial crisis. The interest rate spread is practically non-existent, and it is not coming back any time soon. America enjoyed bursts of growth in the late 20th Century that led to high productivity and growth. After World War II, America had a near monopoly on world manufacturing capacity. America rebuilt much of the world after World War II and satisfied a huge demand for consumer goods. America experienced a twenty-five year period of unprecedented growth which helped the number of credit unions grow to over 21,000 by 1969.

The adoption of the Internet as a means of commerce spurred another growth period. The ability to leverage the efficiencies of technology on a global scale was a major boost for economic growth. The Internet created the means to innovate new business models and enabled people and companies to grow without large capital investments in physical infrastructure. The Internet has been great for economic growth but, unlike the post-war expansion, the Internet also had a negative side for credit unions. New competitors had efficient and convenient access to their members.

It is possible that the development of artificial intelligence technology could cause another growth boost in the future but there are estimates that there will be significant job losses over the next twenty-five years due to the anticipated disruption caused by wide-spread use of artificial intelligence. Many of those disrupted will be credit union members.

The high debt burden of the United States is a huge drag on economic growth. It is now 4% of the GDP and rising. The world's demographics trend to the older side which means more saving and less spending. The economic conditions suggest that the low net interest margin situation is the new normal for the time being.

The world has changed. Credit unions must revise their business model in response. What worked in the 20th Century will not work in the 21st Century.

Scale is King

The credit union's non-profit income tax advantage only helps to a point. Scale is king and picks off the weaker credit unions left and right. Credit unions cannot afford to wait until they grow organically one share account at a time. Credit unions need scale and they need it quickly. There are only three choices for credit unions to grow scale quickly: merge, buy bank assets and collaborate. All three require significant organizational and procedural changes to realize the benefits of scale.

The downside of a merger is that one credit union loses its identity and independence. The merged credit union's brand in the community that was built over many years is gone. In a merger of large credit unions, there is a period of adjustment that requires significant time and resources to work through. Many credit unions merger without a serious effort to reduce employee and infrastructure redundancies which prevents the efficiencies and cost savings the merger was supposed to accomplish.

The challenge of buying bank assets is that it requires a significant cash outlay. You have to transform the bank's culture and convert bank customers into credit union members.

A collaboration between credit unions through a CUSO enables the participating credit unions to remain independent but operate on a larger scale.

Credit unions are no longer disrupters filling a void in the marketplace. Credit unions are being disrupted by FinTech savvy competitors. It is half-time and the coach needs to make changes in how the team plays in the second half or risk losing big time.

Two Survival Questions

It is my opinion that credit unions that want to be competitive and survive will need the following:

a. Technology tools to meet growing member expectations;
b. Data management and analysis tools;
c. The means to contain operational costs;
d. The ability to attract highly capable talent; and
e. Additional income streams that are consumer friendly and not subject to removal by regulation.

My two questions for every credit union are:

a. Does your credit union have the resources, scale and desire to acquire all the above capabilities on its own?

b. If not, what is your plan to grow scale to obtain the necessary resources and expertise?

A credit union's plan to grow scale to meet the competitive pressures is the single biggest strategic issue facing credit unions. The failure to deal with that issue with a sense of urgency is a failure of governance, a potentially fatal failure.

CUSO's

On April 19, 1977, the Federal Credit Union Act was amended to permit credit unions to invest in organizations which are associated with the routine operations of credit unions. The National Credit Union Administration ("NCUA") used this statutory power to pass the first CUSO Regulation in 1979 and revised it in 1986 when Ed Callahan was the Chair of NCUA. The CUSO Regulations has been revised several times since 1986.

It was a different time for credit unions in the 1980's. Car loans were king in the credit union world. Car loan rates in the 1980's were between 10% and 16%. At those rates, credit unions lived very comfortably on the net interest margin. Operational costs were covered and there was enough left over to add to capital. Except for shared branching and ATM networks, credit unions did not need or use CUSO's for operational services. Credit unions were not compelled to find less expensive operational services.

The principal use of CUSO's prior to 2001 was to enable credit unions to receive a share of commission income from broker/dealers in networking arrangements. Due to a regulatory restriction, a credit union could only receive cost reimbursements from third parties. In order to receive the full commission share, the Securities and Exchange Commission ("SEC") permitted credit unions to use CUSO's as the contracting party. CUSO's are not regulated by

NCUA and therefore could be paid a share of commissions. CUSO's became a handy means for credit unions to earn fee income.

In 2001, the regulatory climate changed. The NCUA, under Chairman Dennis Dollar's leadership, passed the Incidental Powers Regulation which permitted credit unions to receive shared revenue from broker/dealers and other third-party vendors. With this change, the SEC required that broker/dealers have the networking arrangements with the credit unions and pay the commission share directly to the credit unions. The reason the SEC wants the credit unions to be the contracting party is that if there is ever an issue with how the investment program is operating in a credit union, the SEC can ask NCUA or the state credit union regulator to intervene to help correct the problem. Since CUSO's are not regulated by NCUA, the SEC does not have a regulator with authority over a CUSO that could compel compliance.

The new rule is that CUSO's can only receive commissions from a broker/dealer if the CUSO is a registered broker/dealer. A handful of CUSO's are registered broker/dealers but most credit unions provide investment service to members through the networking arrangements with a third-party broker/dealer. This subject is covered extensively in my *Guide to Credit Unions Providing Investment and Insurance Services*.

CUSO's were evolving in 2001 and becoming much more important to credit unions than just a legal means to share commissions with a broker/dealer. As the competitive and financial pressures on credit unions increased dramatically, credit unions needed scale to be able to afford growing technology and expertise needs. Credit unions turned culturally and by necessity to collaborative solutions through CUSO's. To reduce their operational cost and obtain higher levels of expertise, credit unions aggregated back-office operations. CUSO's that supported lending operations began to appear for mortgage lending, business lending, and managing the dealer network for indirect auto loans. Credit unions used CUSO's as a means to develop new technologies such as a mobile lending platform and middleware to connect apps to a credit union's core IT.

Wholly owned CUSO's are still widely used by credit unions to provide financial services to members. The most common use of wholly owned CUSO's is to form or buy insurance agencies. Multi-owned CUSO's typically provide operational services to reduce costs. The increase scale of a CUSO makes the technology and expertise much more affordable to the owner credit unions and increases the bargaining power of the credit union owners which tends to lower vendor costs.

Recently, a number of credit union vendors are adding credit unions as co-owners as a means for a vendor to raise capital and/or to attract and retain key credit union clients. Some individual owners of the vendors use a CUSO as a means to sell the business to the credit union clients as part of the individual owners' exit plan. The potential financial return is important but influence over a key service to the credit union seems to be the primary motivation for credit unions buying into a vendor's CUSO.

A few CUSO's have become quite large and impactful in the industry, i.e., PSCU Services, COOP Financial Services, Trellance, and CU Direct. These "Super CUSO's" serve hundreds of credit union clients with critical services at highly competitive costs and are an important part of the credit union industry.

On an annual basis, CUSO's provide multi-millions of dollars in net income to the credit union industry through lower operational costs and additional fee and interest income. As owner/users, credit unions have full alignment with their CUSO's. While difficult to fully quantify, the benefits CUSO's provide to credit unions are enormous. Without CUSO's, each credit union would be isolated with only mergers or buying bank assets as a means to quickly gain scale.

The only data bases on CUSO's are maintained by NCUA in its CUSO Registry (ncua.gov) and by NACUSO in its CUSO Analyzer (nacuso.org). NCUA's CUSO Registry is based on information provided by CUSO's to NCUA. The information NCUA makes available to the public is extremely limited. The CUSO Analyzer on the NACUSO website was developed by Callahan and Associates and has searchable functions on more categories of services and by state, CUSO and credit union investors. You must be a member of NACUSO to access the CUSO Analyzer.

Counting CUSO's and the subsidiaries of CUSO's is not as easy as it may sound. There are CUSO's that are directly owned by credit unions and CUSO's that are subsidiaries of CUSO's that are directly owned by credit unions. The CUSO Analyzer has a little over 1,000 CUSO's and the NCUA CUSO Registry has a little under 1,000 as of 2019. More CUSO's are being formed every month. Our Firm alone forms dozens of new CUSO's every year. Will there be a time that there are more CUSO's than credit unions? Perhaps, but one thing I know for sure is that the credit unions that survive and thrive will leverage the power of collaboration to its fullest and CUSO's will continue to evolve to be more and more integral to the operation of credit unions.

CHAPTER 3
INTRODUCTION TO CREDIT UNION COLLABORATIONS

Credit unions collaborate not because they want to. They collaborate because they have to. We all learned to collaborate in kindergarten. We were taught to share and play nice. The word has a fuzzy, Mr. Rogers kind of sweetness feel. However, for credit unions, collaboration is a business model that is built on enlightened self-interest. Before you think of "us", think of "me." The key to collaboration is to arrange all the "me's" into a functioning "us." What is the self-interest of each credit union partner and how can we align those self-interests in a collaborative business model that is sustainable? A credit union must believe that the collaboration's benefits to the credit union significantly outweigh the time and costs to form and operate the collaboration. It takes a significant amount of time and effort to coordinate services to multiple credit unions. You need positive reinforcement that the effort is worth it.

The fact that collaborations are wide-spread among credit unions and not banks, is caused by two factors. The first is the business necessity. Banks can grow scale by raising capital through stock offerings and credit unions cannot. The second factor is the cooperative model of credit unions which has infused credit unions with a high comfort level with collaborative models. Shared branching and shared ATM networks were early examples of this cultural fit. Successful credit union collaborations often have a bit of an "all for one and one for all" feeling. This cooperative approach tends to be stronger when the collaboration is providing a critical service and when the credit unions are cooperating on multiple services.

The owner/user model is very powerful. You need only to view a credit union business model to see the benefits of a full alignment of interests between credit unions and their members. This is the same alignment that occurs in CUSO's where the credit union users are also the owners. The users provide both the capital and a reliable revenue source for the CUSO. The strategic direction of the CUSO is aligned with the users. The owners are fully engaged to address any service issues. The model has proven itself many times over.

Yes, there are hurdles to collaboration. It is hard work. Entering into a collaboration may mean (a) sharing control of key operational functions with other credit unions; (b) spending significant time on a collaboration with no guaranty of success; (c) entering into collaborative solutions that are not easily reversed; (d) incurring criticism from the board, employees and examiners; and (e) knowing that some employees will lose their job if the full benefits of a collaboration are to be realized. Yet there are credit union pioneers who stepped out and formed CUSO's that today are essential parts of the success of their credit unions.

When considering a collaborative solution, the first and easiest choice is to find an existing collaboration to join.

If an acceptable choice is not available, then consider forming a collaboration.

It is not overstating the situation to say that the competitive threats facing credit unions could cause the eventual demise of credit unions if credit unions do not adapt their traditional business model. When the original thirteen colonies signed the Declaration of Independence, they were facing a life or death situation against a larger and better capitalized foe. Ben Franklin summed up the choice when he said, "We must all hang together, or assuredly we shall all hang separately."

Credit union service organizations ("CUSO's") provide the structure for credit unions to collaborate. A multi-owned CUSO enables credit unions to gather capital and establish the rules for (a) ownership, (b) management rights, and (c) profit and loss sharing. Credit unions that use CUSO's extensively have multiple CUSO relationships, often with overlaps of co-owners in the various CUSO's.

The essential elements of a CUSO is that a CUSO must be a corporation, limited liability company or limited partnership in which a credit union has an ownership interest, and which provides a service permitted by credit union regulations to a customer base which consists primarily of credit unions and/or credit union members. There are several different CUSO ownership/customer types.

Wholly Owned – Single Customer
Credit unions form wholly owned CUSO's to enable them to provide a financial service a credit union does not have the power to provide as a credit union (e.g., non-depository trust services) or is better delivered through a CUSO. For example, a credit union can partner with a third-party insurance agency and receive a share of the commissions on sales to its members if the credit union is

properly licensed, but the credit union cannot fully function as an insurance agency as that is not within the power of credit unions. In the alternative, the credit union can form or buy an insurance agency, which makes the agency a CUSO. The CUSO insurance agency will own the book of business and all the agency commissions, plus have full control over the quality of services.

Wholly Owned CUSO's – Multiple Non-Owner Customers

These are CUSO's that are wholly owned by a credit union but also serves other credit unions as non-owner customers. Typically, these CUSO's are owned by a large credit union that serves smaller credit unions with financial and/or operational services. While there are exceptions, these CUSO's tend not to be as successful because smaller credit unions are slow to recognize the need and undervalue the services offered by a wholly owned CUSO. Small credit unions also fear, sometimes with justification, that a large credit union owner is using a CUSO to target them as a merger candidate.

Multiply Owned – Owner and Non-Owner Customers

These CUSO's serve owner and non-owner credit unions and tend to provide operational services. If the owners are of difference sizes, there may be different classes of ownership. If there are different classes of ownership, the classes tend to have different levels of capital investment and voting rights. These CUSO's tend to provide one type of service; e.g., business lending, compliance, collections, etc.

Multiply Owned – Only Owner Customers ("Co-Sourced")

Co-Sourced CUSO's are solely owned by credit unions and exclusively serve the owner credit unions. The advantage of a CUSO that only serves owners is the perfect alignment of the owner/user model where the owner is incented to solve all service issues. These CUSO's provide operational services and are designed to lower costs and increase expertise. These CUSO's can provide a single service or they can provide multiple services that highly integrate the back-office operations of the owner credit unions.

Collaborations with Entrepreneurs and Vendors

Non-credit unions (entrepreneurs and vendors) may be co-owners of CUSO's. The collaborations can be quite successful but there has to be an acknowledgment that the entrepreneur/vendor will be motivated principally by profit whether from an investment return or by channeling business to the entrepreneur/vendor. The fact that there is a profit motive is not a deterrent. It is just an alignment issue when structuring the CUSO which includes the terms of how the CUSO relationship will be terminated.

Collaborations Without CUSO's

Credit unions have the power to collaborate on some services without a CUSO structure. Credit unions can provide operational services to each other through the Correspondent Incidental Powers. However, without a CUSO, there is no business structure to aggregate capital and share management powers.

The next chapter examines the lessons learned in forming multiply owned CUSO's.

CREDIT UNION COLLABORATIONS

CHAPTER 4
LESSONS LEARNED OVER THIRTY YEARS

I have had a unique perspective over the past thirty years to observe the credit union collaborations first-hand. I have been with credit unions as they plan, implement, modify, expand, and terminate multi-owned collaborations. I recognize why some collaborations succeed and why some fail. The following are twenty-six of the lessons I have learned applicable to CUSO's that have multiple owners.

1. <u>The primary reason to form a collaboration is take advantage of an opportunity to solve a problem.</u> At their essence, collaborations are opportunities to solve problems and credit unions have significant problems to solve. Some might prefer the word "challenges". Creating and maintaining collaborations is hard work and it takes a significant motivator to undertake the effort. The good news is that there are many examples where the hard work has paid off. Collaborations are created by those with the vision to see the challenges to credit unions that lie ahead and understand the urgency to make changes while there is still time to act.

The challenges credit unions face includes insufficient income, too high operating costs, too high vendor costs, insufficient staff expertise, insufficient technology, and lack of access to key service providers. CUSO's provide opportunities to help solve those problems through increasing interest income, increasing fee income, cost reduction/containment of operational costs, obtaining access to key service providers more affordably, and attracting and retaining expertise through enhanced career path opportunities.

2. <u>Clearly define what success will look like</u>. Take the time in the planning stage of the collaboration to define for each credit union (a) the goal for the collaboration (e.g., cost containment and higher expertise levels), (b) the method of achieving the goal (e.g., use of common underwriting criteria and servicing of mortgage loans), (c) the scope of services the collaboration will provide, (d) the service level expectations, and (e) the time-line for implementation and achievement of the goals. These will be your success metrics. Write them down. The business and staffing plan should be written to meet the success metrics.

If your credit union's goal is to save on the costs to originate and service mortgage loans and provide higher levels of expertise, do a base line analysis to measure the cost of your credit union providing those services without a CUSO. Take a survey of the member and staff satisfaction level. Once the CUSO is operational, compare the base line with the CUSO's performance. If you can demonstrate empirically that your CUSO is providing tangible benefits, you will attract other owners and users and the credit union board and examiners will confirm that you are brilliant.

The success metrics will enable you to determine what services will have the "biggest bang for the buck." You will be better able to determine how many partners is an ideal number before the complications of running the collaboration make it counterproductive. For example, an extensive back-office collaboration is complicated to set up and run. There comes a point where adding the complexity of one more owner/user is not worth the marginal savings of the added scale.

3. <u>Calculate the total return</u>. Too often credit unions look at a collaboration as one dimensional, i.e. what has the CUSO paid back in dividends? In determining the full benefit to the credit union, the credit union should consider its total return, which, depending on the type of CUSO could include (a) an investment or patronage return, (b) an increase in capital on the credit union's books based on the appreciation of the CUSO investment value, (c) interest income from loans the CUSO helps the credit union make through expertise and/or technology tools, (d) fee income, (e) the stickiness of a CUSO customer/member (how many more services on average are used by members who use the CUSO for financial services), (f) staff cost savings, (g) vendor cost savings, (h) the value of access to key service providers, and (i) the value of increased staff expertise. Admittedly some of these benefits may be hard to quantify but the value exists. A credit union owner's total return should be identified so that the business model is fairly structured and the partners perceive that they are receiving value in the collaboration.

4. <u>Pick your partners wisely.</u> While a collaboration is formed between credit unions, it is actually formed between people; first the credit union CEO's and then staff and board. Collaboration is hard work even with the best of collaboration partners. Collaboration is impossible with poor partners. The right people make all the difference in the world. How do you find good collaboration partner? Network, network and network some more, especially with peer-sized credit unions. Hang around with

proven credit union collaborators. Attend NACUSO Conferences. I will recommend some partner due diligence questions in the next chapter.

5. <u>Fear is a powerful motivator, but denial helps settle the nerves.</u> People who understand the need to collaborate are able to see the world clearly. They understand that the traditional credit union model of limited loan and deposit services delivered solely in physical branches is obsolete in today's world. They understand that credit unions that do not adjust their business model are on a path of slow-motion liquidation.

Yet many credit unions do not choose to fully use collaborations to reduce costs and increase revenue. Why? Well fear has a role to play in this decision as well. Change does not come naturally to many of our credit union colleagues. Sharing key operational services with another credit union, reducing staff, and offering a new business line can be significant undertakings, especially for smaller credit unions who do not have the staff and resources to research and implement the changes.

It may take a strong denial filter, but many credit unions seem to ignore the obvious. They think this mobile access is a passing fad only teenagers want. Some credit union CEO's know that they have to do something but if they just postpone the hard decisions long enough, they will be retired and it will be someone else's problem. Denial can be a happy place for a while.

6. <u>Collaborations must overcome cultural and instinctive biases.</u> Sharing resources and working together in a collaboration for the mutual benefit of the partners is a concept that is counter to our competitive instincts and the "norms" of business. We have been taught that it is every person for themselves in the business world and we negotiate

in a zero-sum game with winners and losers. Those are not the rules for collaborations. While a collaboration has binding legal documents, the success of a collaboration is not dependent upon the legal terms in a contract, rather it is the power of the owner/user model. If there is a problem for a user, the owner fixes it.

7. <u>The decision to collaborate must overcome the emotional forces that resist change.</u> People have different levels of tolerance for change, from the first-adopter types to the never-over-my-dead-body types. Often the real reasons for the reluctance for change is unspoken. It may even not be fully understood by the person resisting change. We are often called upon to help identify the obstacles to the collaboration and offer recommendations in how to mitigate the concerns. Two colleagues helped me understand the emotional issues in decision making. Tom Davis, past president and director of NACUSO, and professor of industrial psychology, was very insightful. Alan Rush, a consultant to the CUSO, Member Gateways, would be able to read a room full of credit union CEO's, identify the unspoken issues that were impeding the formation of a collaboration and suggested ways of addressing the issues. Alan wrote his doctoral thesis on the "Decision Making of Kings" after interviewing our nation's decision makers at the highest level. Decisions are almost never made on intellectual analysis alone.

8. <u>Educate and communicate with the credit union boards and staff on the reasons for the collaboration and how the collaboration will affect their roles.</u> Making a commitment to significantly change your business model generates responses at a personal and emotional level. Will my status and prestige suffer? Will we be able to keep key employees? What will happen to employees who will be adversely impacted by the changes? Can I truly trust my collaboration partners? If you are going to convince board

members and staff to collaborate, you will need to understand and overcome these personal and emotional obstacles. When change occurs, people want to know why the change is necessary and how the change will affect them. Until those questions are answered, fear and resistance will exist.

9. <u>Trust is the currency of collaborations</u>. Trust means the partners (a) have a shared commitment of the importance and urgency of the collaboration; (b) will timely meet the promises made; (c) will act in the best interest of the other partners; and (d) will regularly communicate to keep the partners aligned. Trust begins with the credit union CEO's and, if successful, moves to the senior staff, the board and the rest of the staff.

10. <u>Champions may create collaborations, but the institutions must sustain them</u>. Credit union CEO's and boards change. The enduring collaborations will develop new champions within the credit unions to ensure their continued success. When credit union boards hire new credit union CEO's, the candidates should be vetted on their commitment to support the collaborations. Over time, the trust factor becomes a part of the institutional DNA between the credit unions.

11. <u>Developing a collaborative mindset opens up new opportunities</u>. Determine what services are off-limits to collaboration (e.g., member facing services) and be open to collaborating on all other services. When new services are considered, think of how new services might be enhanced if done through the collaboration and how that might help both your credit union and your partner credit unions. You will find that you have a host of options to help solve the pressing issues facing your credit union.

12. <u>If the CUSO is providing a key service, hire a CEO level person to run it</u>. Credit unions should not try to

run a CUSO providing a critical service on the cheap. You would not try to run a credit union without a CEO. If the CUSO is run by a person who has to be micro-managed daily by the credit union owners, the CUSO will be mired in mud. Once a capable CUSO CEO is hired, refrain from micromanaging the CEO. The CUSO CEO is accountable to the credit union owner/users but he/she needs the ability to work effectively without excessive interference.

13. <u>A collaboration is a marathon not a sprint.</u> A collaboration will succeed if the partners view the relationship with the lens of the long-term benefits and understand that all services are not "home runs" all the time. Constantly "hitting singles" will win the game. Be patient and understand that set-backs will occur. It will take time to understand how to efficiently blend operations.

14. <u>A collaboration is a relationship not a transaction.</u> Loan agreements are transactions. Service agreements between the credit unions and third-party service providers are transactions. Transactional relationships are a negotiated set of rights and duties that allocate risk and hold the other party responsible for their non-performance. There is an undercurrent of a potential adversarial relationship if things do not go as planned. The well-being of the other party is not a material concern of a party entering into a transactional relationship except as to the ability of the other party to perform as promised.

Credit unions enter into transactional relationships all the time. We lawyers are trained on negotiating agreements to allocate the risks, rights and duties in favor of our clients. It is often a zero-sum situation where risk and duties are pushed back and forth across the negotiating table until an acceptable balance is reached.

CREDIT UNION COLLABORATIONS

Successful collaborations have credit union owners who see the big picture and do not constantly compare their benefits and costs to see who is "winning" and "losing" in the collaboration. That is a transactional mindset and will undermine the collaborative relationship.

As in any successful relationship, the key is to communicate and make adjustments to nurture and strengthen the relationship between the partners and consider the effect of one's actions on the other partners.

15. <u>Scale by itself is not enough</u>. Credit unions are poor at making internal changes in the credit union to fully leverage the benefits of a collaboration or merger. Inserting a CUSO into a credit union's operations can actually add inefficiencies and costs unless the credit union adapts its internal business model to interact efficiently with the services provided by the CUSO. The credit union owners must agree to use the same policies, documents, procedures and related vendors. It is only through standardization of the back-office functions that scale enables the credit unions to achieve the desired efficiencies. Doing more with less people is critical to saving money. This means that credit unions must engage in the unpleasant task of terminating employees who will not be a part of the revised business model.

The strategic thinking must be elevated. A $250 million credit union in a collaboration with three other equal sized credit unions must think in terms of how a credit union with the scale of $1 billion operates. Significant benefits from collaborations require significant changes.

There are four ways to save money in a back-office collaboration; (a) reduce the staff costs, (b) increase the expertise of the staff to be more productive, (c) change the technology, policies, and processes to leverage the increased scale and staff expertise, and (d) be aggressive in vendor selection and negotiations. Without these changes, you are wasting your time with a back-office collaboration.

16. <u>Using scale to drive down vendor costs works dramatically if you forget the golf outing</u>. Do not underestimate the power of scale in negotiation with vendors. This is often the quickest return for a collaboration. To fully realize the benefits of scale all the credit union collaborators must be willing to use the same vendors, forms and procedures. The increased scale and uniformity of the operations is the value that credit unions bring to the vendors and will incent the vendors to slash prices to attract the business. It may take a phase-in period to transfer all credit union owners to a particular vendor, as credit unions may have existing vendor contracts that must expire before they use the CUSO selected vendor.

A very successful CUSO client of ours works with the proposition that any of the top three vendors of a service can provide effective services, so pick one with the best reputation and terms and don't get hung up on the separate bells and whistles that each may have. This CUSO's credit union owners have saved tens of millions of dollars on just the vendor price concessions. The amount of the savings will be much less impressive if a CUSO or credit union picks its vendors based on the number of foursomes bought for the credit union's golf outing.

17. <u>Some collaborations are the collective extensions of the owners</u>. In a Co-Sourced CUSO, the credit union owners co-source operational services to themselves. This concept of credit unions collectively providing services to themselves creates a collaborative extension of the credit unions. The credit unions collectively own and control the CUSO. The services in a Co-Sourced CUSO are not "out-

sourced" which connotes an independent third-party relationship that must be managed quite differently. The distinction between out-sourcing and co-sourcing is critical if credit unions are to maximize the benefits of collaboration.

When a Co-Sourced CUSO does due diligence and makes decisions on operational services, that due diligence and operational decisions should be sufficient for all the owner credit unions to rely upon. If each owner credit union has to do its own due diligence, contract review and decision-making in addition to the Co-Sourced CUSO, the benefits of collaboration have been eliminated. I encourage credit unions and credit union regulators to accept and promote the concept that Co-Sourced CUSO's are the collaborative extensions of the owner credit unions.

There is no need for a Co-Sourced CUSO to bear liability sanctions to make it comply with a service agreement with its owner/users. It makes no sense for the credit union owners to punish themselves collectively through the CUSO in order to motivate the CUSO to solve service problems that they are already incented to solve as users.

A challenge for Co-Sourced CUSO's is that they are swimming against the world view of lawyers and regulators. Lawyers tend to negotiate contracts that put the credit unions in a semi-adversarial position with any party, including a CUSO by treating the CUSO as a third-party vendor. Regulators often look upon Co-Sourced CUSO's as third-party vendors as well.

This is not to say that credit unions do not have a role to play. The credit union owners will establish performance standards for the CUSO that will be monitored and acted upon if the CUSO fails to meet them.

Some of you may ask if my thoughts apply to credit

unions that are clients of a CUSO but not owners and do not have any meaningful input in the management of the CUSO. My answer is no. While all credit unions should expect a CUSO to provide services in a credit union-centric manner, non-owner credit union clients need to treat the relationship with the CUSO as a transaction and negotiate their agreements accordingly.

18. <u>For operational services collaborations, peer-sized credit union partners work best</u>. Peer-sized credit unions face similar problems that require common solutions. Equal voting power works when all the owner/users are of similar size. I have seen numerous examples of successful back-office collaborations with peer-sized credit unions. I cannot say the same for back-office collaborations for disparate sized credit unions. If the credit union owners have different service level expectations, this can create inefficiencies, mismatched pricing and misaligned expectations.

19. <u>Do not try and make revenue on operational services collaborations</u>. Operational services collaborations work when they are designed for cost containment/reduction and increasing staff expertise. Credit unions realize more net income by reducing costs, not from increased revenue from CUSO operations. Conflict arises if some partners change the goal posts in mid-game. For example, some lending services CUSO's have started out by a group of credit unions that agree to share the costs of the needed expertise and thereby reduce their underwriting and servicing costs. Years later people, who may not have been around at the time the CUSO was formed, wonder why the CUSO is not providing profit distributions to the owners. To make a profit to distribute you need to charge the owners more in fees or charge non-owner clients fees with a big profit margin. Neither strategy works well in practice. No owner wants to pay more in fees so the CUSO can turn around and pay them

a distribution. Non-owner clients will not be inclined to use a CUSO that overcharges them. An operational services collaboration works best as a cost containment strategy. As Ben Franklin said, "A penny saved is a penny earned."

However, for every rule there is an outlier. The CUSO, CU*Answers profiled later in the book, has a very successful Co-Sourced Collaboration that provides operational services to many credit unions and pays a dividend based on both the credit union owners' investment and patronage.

20. <u>Consensus management in moderation works but only in moderation</u>. Some credit union CEO's run their credit union by committee. The CEO is not the ultimate "decider." I have heard a CEO say that he wanted to do a particular service, but his staff did not want to proceed so they did not follow through with a CUSO. If everyone is a CEO than no one is the CEO. We need to have a "decider" to keep the ball rolling if consensus does not work. Bringing staff together to integrate a collaboration is tricky business. It is new stuff and everyone has a personal stake in how this will all work out. The cultural changes can be dramatic and, in some cases, traumatic.

A client CUSO created several senior management teams from the three credit union owners to work on the various points of integration: IT support, marketing, compliance, lending, etc. If the teams did not make a decision by consensus, then the three credit union CEO's made a quick and binding decision. So rather than give up the power to decide, the management teams worked out all but a couple of issues themselves. The key was having three credit union CEO's, who were also the directors of the CUSO, on the same page, united in their desire to make the collaboration as effective as possible for the members and not hung up on legacy methods and vendors. The CEO's permitted the consensus process to work to create joint buy-in by the senior management teams with the unspoken message that this collaboration was moving forward with all due haste, so you better get on board now. It worked. One of the credit union CEO's tells me that despite this very lengthy and complicated collaboration process, his credit union has recovered its CUSO organizational costs within the first three years. It is all savings moving forward.

21. <u>Start with a few partners and expand</u>. It is difficult to get a consensus on anything in a large group. I recommend starting a collaboration with no more than two or three partners. Once the collaboration is up and running with an established business model, it is easier to bring other partners into the model. There will not be a forum to nitpick unimportant issues if the train has left the station. Either you get on board or you don't.

22. <u>Collaboration takes patience</u>. The vetting and decision-making process for credit unions is rather slow to put it mildly. It is not unusual for a collaboration to take over nine months from planning to implementation, especially the initial collaboration between credit unions. It is not unusual to begin with six potential collaborators and end up with two or three actual collaborators in a CUSO once the time comes for the credit unions to pull out their wallets to invest.

23. <u>Collaborations are easier once you have a successful one under your belt</u>. The first collaboration will take time to acclimate the stakeholders to the concept. However, once you have a successful collaboration experience, the next one, especially if they involve the same credit union partners, will be much quicker to implement. When choosing the initial service to offer through a collaboration, select one that is easiest to implement. If the initial collaboration is a success, the confidence of the credit

unions will grow to try more ambitious and complicated collaborations.

24. <u>If collaborations are important, have a policy and someone to implement it</u>. Best practices are to have a credit union policy on how the credit union will consider and engage with collaboration opportunities. The policy will provide staff with authority to oversee and implement the policy. There will be a credit union employee with the responsibility to ensure that the agreements with both CUSO's and non-CUSO vendors have agreed service levels that are monitored for compliance. Credit union management and board will not have to guess whether a relationship is meeting expectations. They will have that information available for action if needed. A Sample Collaboration Policy in the Appendix defines the duties of a Collaboration Manager.

25. <u>Just do it</u>. Paralysis by analysis can be a problem. At some point, a collaboration requires a leap of faith grounded on trust. Many successful collaborations have begun when two or three credit union CEO's decide that it is essential to obtain scale. They say to each other, "We have to collaborate and while all the details are not clear yet, we are committed and will find a way." The collaboration will start off with a plan, but the plan is constantly changing as the collaboration faces unforeseen issues. After it is formed, a collaboration requires constant vigilance to measure its effectiveness and keep the partners aligned.

26. <u>Provide a means to unwind a collaboration in whole or in part</u>. Nothing is permanent. Credit unions, boards, CEO's and economic circumstances change. If a partner wants out, the CUSO's bylaws should provide a means for the partner to disassociate. Likewise, if a partner is no longer supporting the collaboration, the other partners need to have the right to involuntarily disassociate the non-

participating partner. A collaboration is healthy if all the participants remain active and engaged. If you do not make clear in the bylaws the financial terms of a disassociation, legal issues can arise. Is the disassociating credit union paid the amount in its capital account or the fair market value of the shares? If fair market value, how are the share valued? Is the payment a lump sum or paid out over time? Make sure the money issues on disassociation are clear.

CREDIT UNION COLLABORATIONS

CHAPTER 5
BUILDING A CUSO BUSINESS MODEL

Keeping in mind the lessons we have learned; the following is my advice on how to structure a multi-owned CUSO so the owners' self-interests align to create a strong collaboration.

<u>Entity Type</u>
Most CUSO's are limited liability companies as LLC's have flexibility in structure and tax advantages for credit unions. I will refer to an LLC model as we discuss collaboration models in this chapter. The LLC owners are called "members" and the board members are called "managers." The members own "units" of the LLC, similar to shares in a corporation. The LLC's "operating agreement" is the equivalent of "bylaws" for a corporation. For obvious reasons, these terms can be confusing. To avoid confusion, I will call the CUSO members "owners", the CUSO managers "directors," the units "shares," and the operating agreement "bylaws".

CUSO's can also be formed as limited partnerships

and corporations. Limited partnerships are rarely used as a credit union has to be a limited partner and not the general partner. As a limited partner the credit union would have limited risk but would not have any management power. For-profit corporations are less flexible than LLC when it comes to creating a customized business structure and corporations are subject to income tax no matter who owns them. Corporations are legally needed for specific CUSO's, such as CUSO's providing non-depository trust services.

Limited liability companies are the preferred form of CUSO entity as LLC's offer the best of corporations and limited partnerships. An LLC can be structured like a corporation and credit union with a board of directors. Credit union representatives can serve on the board and participate in the management of the LLC. An LLC has limited liability to protect the credit union from risks beyond the investment in the LLC. The LLC can be treated as a partnership for tax purposes. There is no income tax at the LLC level. The owners of an LLC pay income tax or not based on the owner's income tax status.

CUSO's can also be non-profit cooperative corporations. Some of the larger CUSO's are cooperatives, PSCU Services, COOP Financial Services, CU Answers and Trellance are examples. They work very well and closely emulate the credit union model of one owner, one vote. The owners are able to earn patronage dividends based on their use of the CUSO's services. The cooperative model does not work when there are unequal management powers, unequal capital investment levels, and investment return expectations.

Define Success and Put It in a Business Plan

We start the planning process with defining the purpose of the collaboration. Each owner will define its own version of success and verify that their definition of success is consistent with the definition of the other owners. Take the time to agree upon and write down (a) the goal for the collaboration, (b) the method of achieving the goal, (c) the scope of services the collaboration will provide, (d) the service expectations, and (e) the time-line for implementation and achievement of the goals. Examine the total expected return or value from the collaboration and make sure the partners agree that the respective returns and value are acceptable. Agree on the success metrics and wrote them down on paper. You may need to remind people of the agreed success metrics at a later time.

What is the scope of the CUSO's services? It is very important to define the precise service so that no false expectations exist. Will the CUSO be the exclusive underwriter and servicer for only first lien purchase money mortgage loans or for all real estate secured loans? Are there any exclusivity exceptions due to the size of the loans or location of the borrower? If the CUSO provides business loan support, will the CUSO collect underwriting information, attend closings and service the loans? If the CUSO is providing compliance services, what portion of the services will be the responsibility of the CUSO and what portion of the services will be the responsibility of the credit unions? Spending time to decide the scope of services will help manage expectations and provide a more realistic business plan.

What are the service expectations of the owners? What are the service metrics that are acceptable as to time and quality of services? One of my CUSO clients set the performance standard of the CUSO at the highest pre-CUSO level among the credit union owners. Of course, to set and measure these standards, you would first have had to measure them at the credit union level. This same CUSO constantly measures its service satisfaction levels and has consistently met or exceeded the agreed service levels.

While it takes some time to measure cost savings and the quality of services, it is time well spent as part of your business plan. The exercise will enable you to defend the value of the CUSO to examiners or board members. You should have service level agreements with your CUSO just as you would with any vendor to ensure that both the credit union owners and the CUSO personnel have the same service expectations. If the expectations are not met, then the credit union owners can make adjustments as necessary.

How long will it take to reach these goals and service levels? How much investment and staff will it take? What are the assumptions on revenue and expenses and the implementation time frame? All this information goes into a business plan that is refined and approved by the credit union owners.

The process of developing the business plan may or may not require a subject matter expert or facilitator. If there is a cost associated with the process, I suggest a Feasibility Agreement. Each prospective owner throws in a sum of money which is used to pay the costs of the feasibility study. If a prospect chooses not to invest in the CUSO, the funds are forfeited. Think of it as tuition costs. If a CUSO is formed, the funds can either be expensed by the credit unions joining the CUSO or capitalized as a pre-formation cost.

Examine the Risks

A CUSO is a risk sharing vehicle. Not all projects will be winners. Some may lose money. Better to share in the risks than having your credit union assume them alone. Risk sharing through collaboration enables credit unions to take larger business risks that may lead to a larger upside.

In a multi-owned operational services CUSO, the financial risk is low. There is a built-in customer base that is motivated to remain a customer. The owner/users are already paying for the service internally. They are re-directing funds that are already being spent internally to a CUSO providing the same operational service. The plan is to reduce the credit union's financial burden through a CUSO that is already being carried by the credit union.

Capital Levels

The business plan will indicate how much capital is needed for the CUSO to become self-sustaining. I recommend that the credit unions fund the CUSO at least at this capital level. By doing so, the CUSO will be adequately funded to be financially independent of the credit unions. Having a CUSO with sufficient capital to be financially independent strengthens the CUSO's corporate veil liability protection. I recommend that credit unions invest more than the minimum capital amount or provide lines of credit to cover cash flow and unforeseen contingencies. While cash flow concerns are not usually an issue for a well-capitalized credit union, CUSO's sometimes have cash flow issues. Take cash flow into consideration as a factor in the capital level decision. Business plans never go off perfectly and the last thing you want to do is to go back to the credit union board for more funding.

Some entrepreneurs/vendors bring their company and know-how to a CUSO and are awarded shares for their "in-kind" contribution. In other words, they bring the expertise and the credit unions bring the cash. The number of shares that are awarded for this in-kind contribution, is subject to negotiation. In some cases, the credit unions receive their cash investment back through distributions prior to making distributions to the owners who do not invest cash.

Who has responsibility for additional capital contributions, if needed? In the typical model the responsibility falls on the owners, proportionate to their respective ownership interests. In some CUSO's that responsibility can fall upon one class of owner, usually the owners with the most invested capital and voting power. As the NCUA CUSO Regulations require a credit union approves a CUSO investment and there are limits to a credit union's power to invest in CUSO's, we do not require a credit union to write a blank check. Any additional capital investment request is subject to the credit union's approval.

Some services such as technology development, require a constant infusion of capital. The restrictions on a credit union's power to invest in CUSO's and the inability to commit a credit union to invest, can cause capital sufficiency issues in CUSO's that are capital intensive.

NCUA does not regulate a CUSO so there are no restrictions on how a CUSO may invest its excess cash not currently needed for operations. However, NCUA will not permit a CUSO to be the means for a credit union to make investments that are not permitted for credit unions. The question turns on the intent, source and purpose of funds. Credit unions cannot make investments in a CUSO solely to make impermissible investments. However, a CUSO's excess operating funds, especially funds earned by the CUSO, have no investment restrictions.

Income Tax Issues

The income tax issue is more important for those CUSO's have income producing goals as opposed to CUSO's that are expense sharing collaborations. A principal reason for the popularity of the limited liability company entity is that there is no income tax obligation at the LLC level. The proportionate income tax obligation is passed through to the owners. If an owner owns a 25% interest in the CUSO, the owner receives a K-1 for 25% of the net taxable revenue each year. A credit union owner does not have to pay income tax on the taxable revenue assigned to the credit union on the K-1 but the credit union may have to pay unrelated business income tax ("UBIT"). UBIT is essentially an income tax on the portion of the income that is not related to the non-profit's charitable purpose. For example, many hospitals are organized as non-profits. When the non-profit hospitals opened fitness centers, the owners of for-profit fitness centers complained to Congress that the hospitals had an unfair tax advantage providing a service that is not central to their charitable purpose. Consequently, Congress created UBIT to tax the net revenue the hospital received from their fitness centers.

Only state-chartered credit unions face the possibility of paying UBIT. Federally-chartered credit unions are considered "federal instrumentalities" that are not obligated to pay either income tax or UBIT. Whether a state-chartered credit union is obligated to pay UBIT on its share of revenue from a CUSO depends on the services and the customers. The First Community Credit Union case in Wisconsin in 2009 and the Bellco Credit Union case in Colorado in 2009 and 2010 established some guidance. In order for the income from financial services not to be taxable as UBIT, the services generating the income have to have been provided to the credit union's members and the services have to be related to the general fiscal thrift purposes for which credit unions were created to serve. The cases held that credit life and disability insurance, GAP coverage, AD&D insurance and networking fees the credit union receives from an affiliated broker/dealer serving members were exempt from UBIT. Services to non-members are subject to UBIT as was income that could not be traced to a member service.

If an entrepreneur or for-profit company is a co-owner of a CUSO, they will have to pay income taxes on their portion of the net taxable revenue. Often the bylaws call for the annual distribution of funds to them to pay their income taxes arising from their ownership of shares in the CUSO. Sometimes the bylaws require that the distributions to non-credit union owners trigger proportionate distributions to the credit union owners. Of course, no distributions can be made if there are not sufficient funds over and above expenses and reserves to pay them.

Pricing
The best practice for a CUSO designed to contain operational costs is to set the fees at a level that covers the cost of the services plus a contingency reserve. Should owners receive price concessions over non-owner clients? I am not a fan of CUSO's charging non-owners a premium over owners. It seldom works. If the fees to non-owners are more than market rates, that strategy will not last long as the non-owners will look elsewhere for services. The best practice is to use the same fee schedule for all clients. The owners will still benefit as the extra volume provided by the non-owners should lower the costs to the CUSO. Aggressive owner price concessions can lead to cash flow issues. I have seen CUSO's have to recapitalize when overly generous owner price concessions were made.

Some CUSO's use tiered pricing. The more revenue a credit union generates, the cost per service is reduced. Tiered pricing has merit. The scale created by the credit unions making significant contributions to revenue is good for all the owners and the price breaks serve as an incentive to those owners generating large amounts of revenue to remain in the CUSO. If you use tiered pricing, make sure that the price breaks are above the revenue levels needed to cover the cost of services.

Staffing
Many multi-owned operational CUSO's begin with using experienced credit union employees to work for the CUSO part-time. The CUSO reimburses the credit union

for an employee's time by estimating the percentage of time the employee spends on CUSO business and applying that percentage to the employee's salary and cost of employee benefits. While it is desirable for the CUSO to have full-time employees, the practical issues of HR and the administration of employee benefits often results in the use of a credit union as the W-2 employee until the CUSO's scale and employee count increases.

If you want the CUSO to run well, appoint someone with the sole or primary duty to do so. CUSO's that are run part-time by a busy credit union executive rarely gets the management attention the CUSO needs to succeed.

When lending employees from the credit union to the CUSO on a part-time basis, have an agreement in place that clearly states the terms of the arrangement as if the credit union and CUSO were unrelated third parties. You do not want to jeopardize the corporate veil between the credit union and CUSO that protects the credit union from negligent acts caused by the CUSO and its employees. I recommend having a term in the employee sharing agreement that states when the shared employee is performing tasks for the CUSO, the employee is under the sole management of the CUSO and not the credit union. Make sure the shared employee represents that he or she is working for the CUSO when acting in that capacity. The name on contracts, email addresses, letterhead and business cards needs to be the CUSO's name when CUSO business is conducted. Judges are reluctant to pierce the corporate veil protections but do not give a plaintiff ammunition to do so. While I provide these stern warnings, credit unions and CUSO's have a long history of sharing employees without liability issues accruing to the credit union owner for the negligence of the CUSO.

Owners
Owners should be added with deliberate thought.

What characteristics qualify a credit union for ownership? Choose your fellow owners wisely. Alignment of purpose and personalities between credit union partners is an important success factor.

In the Co-Sourced Model, peer-sized credit unions are the sole owners. Some CUSO's service credit union owners of different sizes. These CUSO's often have different classes of ownership. Classes of ownership (e.g., Class A Owners and Class B Owners) are used to reflect differences such as the minimum capital contribution, the power to vote, the power to appoint directors, and/or profit sharing.

Some CUSO's, particularly CUSO's providing technology services, find they need to provide equity to employees as an incentive in order to compete with other companies for highly talented employees. These employees usually own a class of shares that does not have voting rights. The percentage of shares available to employees is usually kept small (under 10%) so that the return to the credit unions contributing capital is not overly diluted.

A CUSO can be owned 100% by credit unions or 1% by credit unions. Note that it is the customer base that has to be primarily members or credit unions. Non-credit union owners are permitted. Some state-chartered credit unions have rules regarding non-credit unions owners. In Oregon, a state-chartered credit union may invest in a CUSO only if its majority ownership consists of credit unions. In California, a state-chartered credit union may invest in a CUSO co-owned by a non-credit union if the state credit union regulator consents to the investment.

CUSO's offer a means for innovators and entrepreneurs to enter the credit union industry and partner with credit unions. The use of CUSO's tends to accelerate the entrepreneur's penetration of the credit union market.

Sometimes you have an entrepreneur who formed a company that credit unions later invested in, rendering the company a CUSO. The entrepreneur may have decided to add credit union partners to acquire capital or to gain better market penetration and client "stickiness." Credit unions tend to prefer working with CUSO's as credit union ownership keeps the company better aligned with the interests of the credit union customers. The potential to earn additional income is important but is often secondary to the ability of the credit union owners to influence the services provided.

Typically, the entrepreneur will have his or her own class of ownership that will provide a controlling management position. The entrepreneur will have a profit goal and/or capital appreciation goal. The credit unions need to understand and accept that their interest will be partially, but not totally aligned, with the entrepreneur. If there is a profit goal, the credit union owners will usually share in that profit. The entrepreneur will typically, but not always, need a cash-out exit strategy which means the credit union buys him/her out or the CUSO is sold to a third party.

Due to the incomplete alignment of interest between the entrepreneur and the owner/user credit unions, care must be given to provide the means for credit unions and the entrepreneur to part ways in a manner that is fair to both sides. Given the profit component, expect that the purchase price for the shares will be at fair market value. There are examples of very successful CUSO's that are co-owned by entrepreneurs. The entrepreneur and credit union owners have thought through the issues specific to these types of CUSO's and created terms in the agreements that work for them.

Partner Due Diligence

The good news is that you seem to have a collaboration service you want to deploy and have identified potential partners. How do you know that the partner will be an effective co-collaborator? Let's ask some questions about your potential partners and maybe yourself as well.

Do your partners view the collaboration as essential to their success? We collaborate because we must in order to survive and be successful. If your partner is not of the same mindset, the collaboration may not last. Full commitment to a collaboration is necessary for long-term success and a healthy dose of the fear of going out-of-business helps to focus the mind and create commitment.

Does your partner view the collaboration as a transaction or a relationship? Can your partner focus on the long-term relationship and the actions necessary to accomplish the core goal? Credit unions that focus on the short-term benefits for themselves are poor partners. A partner that has an attitude of "what have you done for me lately," is not a partner for the long term.

Can the partner tolerate short term failures and multiple adjustments to correct the failures? Innovation and collaboration enjoy success but often it comes with multiple failures along the way. Collaboration is a process of planning, implementation, enjoying some success, enduring some failure, and making constant adjustments until a successful model is built. If the partners are committed to their core goals, they will find a way to meet those goals, but it does not usually happen from day one. Are they able to give their staff the freedom to try and fail? A well-analyzed failure is an investment in learning how to be successful.

Can the partners reward results and not tolerate mediocrity? Collaborations must be merit based. Employees and vendors who produce results that contribute to the success of the collaboration are rewarded and those who do not must be separated from the collaboration. Successful collaborations are transparent and strictly accountable on performance and costs to their credit union partners and they must behave that way.

Is the partner open to innovation and new ideas to solve old problems by looking outside the credit union industry for ideas? The "we have always done it that way" mindset has no place in collaborations. Find those partners who dare to be different.

Can the partner share control of critical operational services? This is hard to do for some but the ability for a partner credit union to do this is essential. This needs to be vetted with both the CEO and the board of the partner credit union.

Can the partners make internal changes in their credit unions to leverage the collaboration? To obtain the benefits of a collaboration a partner credit union may have to reduce staff, change vendors and/or change internal operating processes. If the partner credit union is unwilling to do so, the cost savings will not be as great for the partner and the partner may not be as keen on fully supporting the collaboration over time.

Do I trust my partner? Trust begins with the CEO's of the credit union. Do your head and your gut tell you that your fellow CEO will be there when times get tough and stick by you and the collaboration? Do you see anything in the partner credit union that gives you a concern that your partner CEO could be undermined by his/her staff or board when problems arise? Does the CEO have the confidence of his/her board to act without being micro-managed?

What is the "currency" of the CEO? Allan Cohen and Dave Bradford in their book *Influence Without Authority* discuss how to work in situations where you do not have organizational control over colleagues to accomplish your goals. The book advises the reader to discover your colleague's "currency." What does your colleague need and how can you help deliver on those needs so your colleague will help you? If your partner's currency is to accomplish the same goals for his or her credit union as you are seeking for your credit union, then trading is easy. If the currency is inconsistent with the collaboration's goals, the trade becomes more difficult to manage. Are there issues within the partner credit union that concerns your partner CEO? Does your partner CEO have personal goals that may conflict with your goals? Are you able to aid the partner CEO without adversely affecting the collaboration and your currency? The key is to know all the pressures and opportunities affecting your partner so you know how to manage the challenges in the relationship. You can't manage what you do not know.

Will the CEO and staff be able to enforce decisions? Consensus is nice but consensus on all issues takes time and is always at risk of sabotage by a few staffers reluctant to change. Collaborations need decisive decision making from time to time to keep it going and to compel the staff to get on board or exit the bus. If everyone shares the power of the CEO to make or block business decisions, then there is no CEO and no leadership.

Will your partner be able to stick with decisions despite outside criticism? Many people specialize in criticizing change, any change. Like most business plans, there are short term disruptions and costs in order to realize long term gains. Criticism can come from an examiner, a dissident board member, industry colleagues or a disgruntled staff member. If you have a good plan, you must have the fortitude to stay on plan. Make sure your partners have the same level of determination.

How supportive are the boards and senior staff? Strong board support is essential to the success of collaborations. There must be a high trust factor in the credit union staff and boards in order to commit to common platforms for critical services. While the CEO to CEO relationship is the most critical, there needs to be a socialization process and interaction between the boards of the credit unions for extensive Co-Sourced collaborations. The credit union directors should meet and get to know each other on a personal basis. For Co-Sourced CUSO's it is common to have annual joint planning sessions. If a collaboration is a one-service and one-off situation, there is less need for this level of socialization.

Are our decision-making processes and timing compatible? Credit unions differ on how they make decisions and how long that process takes. If your partner makes decisions at a snail's pace, they may not have the ability to timely adapt to changing conditions. It is very helpful if each CEO has similar decision-making authority that they can implement without board approval.

Does my partner have sufficient resources and time to meet an agreed implementation plan? Good intentions aside, does the partner credit union and the CEO have the financial and people resources to timely hold up their end of the bargain? Are there any issues on their plate that will adversely affect the collaboration's implementation schedule?

The credit union CEO's will change. What happens when the CEO's change? If the collaboration provides a critical service that the partner credit unions rely upon, how can we assure ourselves that a new CEO will not come in and upset the apple cart? The partner credit unions must institutionalize the collaboration within the credit unions. Personal relationships must be formed between the credit union staff and between the credit union directors. When a new credit union CEO is hired, the board of that credit union should vet the candidates for the CEO position to see how compatible the candidates are with the collaboration.

Collaborations offer tremendous opportunity to succeed. Partner credit unions who understand that are motivated partners. Can your partner get excited about the potential of collaboration? It is more fun and exciting to hang with an enthusiastic crowd.

Owner Transition Issues
How do you add partners that will benefit the collaboration and separate from partners in a manner that is not disruptive to the collaboration and be fair to all concerned? You need to create a door out of the collaboration with rules. Collaboration partners will not last forever. The failure to deal with disassociation issues in the bylaws can lead to costly disputes.

My recommendation is to permit a credit union to withdraw from a CUSO after notice. The notice can be relatively short (30 days) or long (180 days) depending on the service and the practical issues associated with the departure of the credit union. It is also my recommendation to give the owners the ability to terminate the ownership of a credit union that is no longer using the services of the CUSO. The power of collaboration is that everyone is contributing and if a credit union ceases to be a contributor and refuses to leave on its own, the other owners need to have the option to compel the disassociation of that credit union after notice and the credit union's election not to re-engage as a participant.

In both a voluntary and non-voluntary disassociation,

I recommend paying the disassociating credit union its capital account balance on the date of its disassociation. The payment may be made over a period (usually two to five years) without interest. The deferred payout prevents a cash flow issue for the CUSO and the payment of the balance in the capital account helps prevent legal issues with the disassociating credit union. As a CUSO owned by credit unions providing operational services to themselves is not designed to make a profit, we do not have to worry about blue-sky values. I note that some CUSO's require a disassociating owner to forfeit its capital account balance. While a credit union would have to accept the forfeiture if that term was in the bylaws, I think it is an impediment to obtaining investors.

The situation is different if the CUSO is designed to generate net income and the purpose is to grow equity value. This is especially true where there are non-credit union owners. In those cases, a payout of a net capital account will not be sufficient. Fair market values will have to be established through past share sales or by expert appraisals.

If key employees are provided shares, the CUSO usually has the option, but not the obligation to buy back the shares once the employee ceases to be an employee. The buyout may be the fair market value of the shares or a formula of the increase in equity during the employee's tenure, e.g., a value based on the increase in the CUSO's gross or net revenue.

Management
Multi-owned operational CUSO's are managed by a board. If the CUSO is owned by credit unions of near equal size, the board is typically comprised of one director for each owner. The directors are typically the CEO or a senior staff of the credit union owner. If the CUSO's services are critical to the credit union owner, it is important to have the owner

CEO's involved in the management of the CUSO, at least at the outset of operations. You want to have directors with the power to make important decisions without "checking back" with others at their credit union.

If a multi-owned operational CUSO has credit union owners of significantly unequal size, you can have different classes of ownership with the smaller credit unions either having little or no voting rights and little or no ability to appoint or elect directors. You want to have a manageable board size. I have seen as many as eleven directors for some large CUSO's but the typical number is five or seven. Sometimes the large investors each appoint a director and the small investors collectively elect one director. You can customize the board as necessary to attract owners, users and capital.

You can use several techniques to customize management control. You can use weighted votes. Owner votes are almost always weighted by the number of shares owned. You can also weight director votes by the number of shares owned by the owner appointing the director. This method enables an owner that has 60% management control and owns 60% of the shares to appoint one director on a board of five who exercises majority control through weighted voting without the need to elect three of the five directors. As a result, there is room for more owners and voices on the board without the board becoming too large.

You can use different levels of consent. Some matters may require super majority or unanimous consent. Some matters are decided by the owners and some by the board. Most CUSO's like to keep as much power in the board as possible as it is more efficient. If all owners are represented on the board and the votes are weighted, there is no reason to have separate owner votes as the voting power is the same. However, if all owners are not represented on the board, a fundamental matter, such as a vote to change the terms in the bylaws, will usually require a vote by the owners. If the number of owners is three or less, I recommend unanimous consent to change the bylaws. Over three owners, I recommend a super majority consent at a level of 75%. I have seen situations where the consensus of multiple owners is frustrated by the actions of a single owner because unanimous consent was required to resolve the issue in question.

There are CUSO's that were started by a single credit union and other credit union owners were added later. Sometimes the founder does not want to give up control. This is generally not advisable in the long run as the CUSO will not attract peer-sized credit unions if they will always be junior partners and not co-equal partners, especially if the collaboration involves a critical service. Co-managing a critical service is hard but doable. Having another credit union control a critical service is a non-starter. Even if the founding credit union wants to maintain a controlling interest through the transition period, it is my recommendation that the control be relinquished and shared after a period of time.

Some CUSO's have advisory boards to provide a forum for customer feedback from those credit unions that do not have board representation. The advisory boards do not have any management powers.

Profit and Loss Sharing

When forming a CUSO that is expected to provide an investment return, the profit and loss sharing terms in the bylaws become an important term. The traditional investment return model is that net profits are distributed per the percentage of shares owned. That is the model for some CUSO's. Other CUSO's want to have an incentive to drive business to the CUSO. An owner/user has two points of value. The first is the percentage of capital contributed. The second is the amount of business driven by the owner to the CUSO, usually measured by gross revenue. In order to incent the credit union to drive more business to the CUSO, some CUSO's have a patronage return component along with an investment return. For example, if a CUSO's board declares a dividend distribution, the bylaws may state that 50% of the distribution is paid per the proportion of shares owned and 50% is paid per the proportionate gross revenue generated from the owner as compared to other owners since the last patronage distribution.

Tiered pricing is an alternative to a patronage dividend. The more services a credit union buys, the lower the fee per service. This works as long as the discounted prices are above the CUSO's cost of providing the services. Tiered pricing can be implemented in CUSO's that are both for-profit business models and cost containment models. Patronage dividends will only work if the CUSO is designed to generate profits and make distributions. However, patronage dividends can be more effective in managing cash flow. The board decides when it is financially prudent to make patronage dividends. Keep in mind there are laws, such as RESPA, that must be considered in how you can legally incent credit unions for referrals in some lines of business.

There are two reasons for rewarding credit unions for their relative levels of support in driving revenue to the CUSO. The first reason is to incent the owners to contribute to the scale and success of the CUSO for the benefit of all the owners. The CUSO was formed with the assumption that the credit unions would support the CUSO at a level consistent with the business plan that will achieve the desired benefits from economies of scale. The CUSO is a collaboration and each party in the collaboration must contribute to its full potential or the enterprise is less effective. The second reason is to incent the larger contributors to stay in the CUSO. If you have parties contributing business at different levels but receiving the same reward, you run the risk that the party that is making significantly more contributions may decide to leave the CUSO for other opportunities.

Consider the total return from the collaboration as previously discussed in Chapter 4 and make sure all owners agree on how the financial benefits will be realized. Differing views on how and when financial benefits will be distributed cause rifts among the owners.

Holding Company Model

In situations where a credit union owns multiple CUSO's, there are credit unions that own their multiple CUSO's through a single Holding Company CUSO. In other words, the credit union owns a single CUSO and that CUSO is the owner of the subsidiary CUSO's that provide services to members and/or credit unions. Under NCUA's rules, a subsidiary CUSO has the same compliance and reporting requirements as a CUSO owned directly by a credit union.

The profits earned by CUSO's can be better leveraged using a Holding Company CUSO by keeping the funds outside of the credit union. If the credit union is the direct investor in all its CUSO's, its aggregate CUSO investment limit will apply each time the credit union makes a new CUSO investment. For example, if a credit union directly owns a mortgage CUSO and an insurance CUSO and wants to increase the investment in the insurance CUSO by using the profits from the mortgage CUSO, the credit union could take a dividend from the mortgage CUSO and then make a direct investment in the insurance CUSO. The credit union would have to comply with the aggregate CUSO investment limitation in doing so as the investment is coming from the credit union. However, if the credit union had a holding company model, the mortgage CUSO would dividend the funds to the Holding Company CUSO and the Holding Company CUSO would make the additional investment in the insurance CUSO. Since the funds never went into the credit union, there is no aggregate credit union investment limit to consider.

In the above example, the mortgage CUSO could have made a direct investment in the insurance CUSO but that would not work if the mortgage CUSO were owned by other credit unions and the insurance CUSO was wholly owned. You would not want to add other credit union owners not involved with your insurance CUSO as indirect owners.

For credit unions using the Holding Company CUSO model with all limited liability company CUSO's, the profits and losses from the subsidiary CUSO's roll up to the credit union through the Holding Company under GAAP just as they would if the credit union owned the subsidiary CUSO's directly.

Holding Company CUSO's also are the means by which credit unions manage all their CUSO's. There are advantages of consolidating common management and administrative services in the Holding Company CUSO that support all CUSO operations. The board of directors and management of the credit union have one entity to deal with and hold accountable on CUSO issues. As NCUA does not have a "holding company" as a permitted service, we often list the services for the Holding Company as management services.

In the Holding Company CUSO, the typical governance model would be to have some board overlap between the Holding Company CUSO and the subsidiary

CUSO's. For example, you might have five board members at the Holding Company CUSO level, all of whom are senior staff of the credit union and appointed by the owner credit union's board. The Holding Company CUSO would be the sole investor in two subsidiary CUSO's. In our example, the insurance services CUSO may have a board consisting of the manager of the insurance services, an outside person who has insurance expertise and three board members from the Holding Company CUSO board. The mortgage services CUSO board would be similarly structured. In this manner, you would have a Holding Company CUSO board that controls all subsidiary CUSO operations with added expertise for the particular services provided by the subsidiary CUSO's.

A representative of the Holding Company CUSO would be the liaison with the credit union board on CUSO matters to keep them informed and to coordinate the CUSO services to better serve the credit union and its members. I recommend that the credit union CEO serve on the Holding Company CUSO board and be the CUSO liaison to the credit union board.

Some may ask why not run all the services out of the same CUSO? Absent a reason to separate business in different CUSO's, I agree that you can keep some multiple businesses in the same CUSO. The following are reasons to separate services in different CUSO's:

1. Due to regulations, the services can only be delivered in a single purpose CUSO.
2. The CUSO provides a highly regulated service and you do not want the complications of running other services out of the same CUSO.
3. There are different owners for the different services, or you plan to bring in additional owners for some but not all the services in the future. You do not

want the complication of having a mismatch of owners and users in the same organization.
4. A service may have a high-risk factor that you want to isolate from other services so they are not adversely affected by the high risk.

Expansion of Ownership

You have a CUSO and now you want to expand the ownership. In deciding whether to expand ownership the first step is to determine your goal. If it is to bring in new capital, do you have a plan in place to use the capital? Taking in capital entails a responsibility to use the capital in a productive manner. A business plan will lay out the use of the capital. If the expansion is to attract and retain good credit union partners who will also be "stickier" clients of the CUSO, then the selection of good partners is essential. Usually the goals will involve both capital and client expansion.

All money is not green. If the new partners are not compatible with your credit union, the cost of taking them on will far outweigh the benefits of their capital contribution. Take time for the key people in the owners to meet personally and develop trust on a personal level, the only level that matters.

The mechanics of the offering is straightforward. You will need (1) a business plan for three to five years; (2) revised bylaws to reflect any structural changes to accommodate the expansion of ownership; (3) a subscription or admission agreement; (4) a sample NCUA required attorney opinion letter on the credit union investor's legal risks; (5) a sample services agreement between the CUSO and its clients; and (6) any employment agreements with CUSO employees. In most cases, I also recommend a private placement memorandum setting forth the terms of the offering and the investment risk. The offering should indicate the ability of the CUSO to modify or extend the terms of the offering. You will need to decide upon the total offering amount, the per share price and the time frame for the solicitation. As almost all CUSO share offerings are to a limited number of credit unions that are accredited and institutional investors, the securities registration exceptions apply.

Some CUSO's seek professional assistance through their accountants or an industry expert to set a share price. Some CUSO's back into the share price based upon the capital needs and some just set the price by what they think the market will bear. Usually there is a premium over the initial share price paid by the founders, if the CUSO has become a self-sustaining on-going operation.

Most solicitations are not open-ended but have a time limitation. The time limitation serves several purposes. First, it provides a time limit for credit unions to make decisions. We all know how some credit unions can procrastinate. Having said that, the time limit should not be too short as the credit unions will have to have time to do due diligence and take the investment offering to their boards for approval. Credit union boards rarely act on a matter the first time they see it. Second, you do not want the share price to be stagnant without an opportunity to review and modify the price over time. Third, you want to have a definite time set to use the proceeds of the solicitation to meet the business plan. If the solicitation is undersubscribed after the end of the solicitation period, you will want to re-evaluate the terms of the solicitation or the feasibility of the business plan. If you do change the business plan because the subscription is undersubscribed, you will have to obtain the permission of the investors to proceed with a revised plan because they invested with an understanding that the business plan presented to them was to be implemented.

The safest course of action is not to use the proceeds of the solicitation until the subscription is fully subscribed. If you use the investments as they come in, you run the risk of an unhappy investor if the subscription is not filled and the business plan is not implemented after you have spent the investor's money. However, there are situations where the solicitation is open-ended, and investments are used as contributed. If that is the case, make sure the investors are informed of this.

Vendor Created CUSO's

Some credit union vendors desire to form CUSO's. The reason may be to attract low cost capital, tie credit unions to the vendor's services and/or provide a means to buy-out the individual owners of the vendor. Credit unions desire to be owners in order to have influence and input into a key service provider, lower service fees, receive dividends, and/or receive a share of the sales proceeds if the vendor is sold to a third party.

If the vendor is providing a service permitted by the CUSO Regulation (as is likely the case if the vendor provides a type of operational services) and primarily serves credit unions and has no plans to change the customer base, the credit unions can invest in the vendor directly. If the vendor does not primarily serve credit unions or has plans to grow the non-credit union business, a direct investment in the vendor will not qualify as a permitted CUSO investment. The solution is for the vendor to form a subsidiary which will exclusively serve the credit union market. Credit unions may invest along with the parent vendor in this subsidiary. The subsidiary is a CUSO by virtue of the credit unions' investment. The CUSO will market to credit unions and contract with the credit unions to provide the vendor services. The CUSO usually subcontracts the performance of the services to the vendor. The vendor will own any intellectual property rights and sub-licensed the rights to the CUSO.

In soliciting investment, vendors usually have a third-party evaluate the fair market value of the shares. The investment terms are set forth on a term sheet that is vetted with the vendor's key credit union clients. Once the terms are agreed to in principle, the bylaws and investment documents are prepared and circulated.

Typically, the vendor retains control of the day-to-day operation of the CUSO but credit union representatives serve on the CUSO's board. Usually a portion of the credit union representatives are required to consent to changing the terms of the bylaws, any agreements between the CUSO and the vendor, and the admission of new members. It is also typical that the credit union owner has to remain a customer of the vendor to continue to be an owner of the CUSO. In some cases, a credit union representative will serve on the vendor's board of directors.

This arrangement may mean that the credit union owners of the CUSO would not be able to benefit from the sale of the vendor. This seems unfair as the credit unions helped build the vendors' business and are not permitted to be an owner of a vendor directly due to a regulatory restriction. In order for the credit union owners of the CUSO to benefit from a sale of the vendor to a third party, the credit unions will typically be provided warrants by the parent vendor exercisable immediately prior to the sale of the parent vendor.

Often there are drag-along rights and tag-along rights. Drag-along rights is when a majority owner can compel the minority owners to sell as long as the minority owners are receiving the same proportionate terms in the sale. Drag-along rights are needed if the buyer wants to buy 100% of the company. Tag-along rights is when a majority owner is selling its interest to a buyer and the minority owners want to tag along with the majority upon the same proportionate terms. Tag-along rights are used when the buyer is only seeking to buy a majority interest in the company. This means the majority owner cannot sell unless the buyer agrees to buy the electing minority owners' interest as well.

CHAPTER 6
NACUSO

The National Association of Credit Union Service Organizations ("NACUSO") is the trade association for credit union service organizations. It's voting members are CUSO's and credit unions. It's non-voting members are vendors serving credit unions and CUSO's.

The organizers of NACUSO first met in a conference room at the San Francisco Airport in 1985. Most of the organizers were from California. One reason John Unangst was recruited for the NACUSO Board was that he lived east of the Mississippi.

Bob Dorsa was one of the original organizers and the first President of NACUSO. He served from 1985 to 2005. This was during the period of time that CUSO's were primarily used as the means for credit unions to work with broker/dealers to provide investment services to credit union members. Bob is from Long Island, New York but moved to

California to work at Litton Credit Union as a mortgage lender. As president of NACUSO, Bob created good working relationships with the broker/dealers serving the industry. He also worked very hard to give the conference attendees a great experience. He sought out good speakers and insisted on first rate food and beverage.

NACUSO had a low overhead model dependent upon fees from conferences sponsored by the broker/dealers serving the industry. The cost of speakers was low, using attendees for breakout sessions and only paying a keynote speaker. Bob and Guy filled in the rest.

When Incidental Powers Regulations was passed in 2001 and CUSO's were no longer used for investment services networking arrangements, the NACUSO business model was revised. With NACUSO's consent, Bob was also running the American Credit Union Mortgage Association. Bob decided to dedicate his effort full time to ACUMA in 2005. He has since built ACUMA into a vibrant trade association that supports credit union mortgage lending.

As the NACUSO Board considered how it would re-invent itself, a new president was needed. The Board asked Board Member Vic Pantea to take the job. Vic made the strategic mistake of leaving the room when the Board decided that he should be President. To his credit, he accepted the position. Vic is a former credit union executive and was serving as President of Member Gateways at the time. Member Gateways was a CUSO of twenty plus large credit unions that identified and funded scalable technology driven member services. Member Gateways gave Vic the green light to also serve as NACUSO's President.

Vic changed the NACUSO business model. He solicited about a dozen large CUSO's to pay an annual subscription of $20,000 for the status of a Platinum Partner Membership. A Platinum Partner Membership gave the CUSO preferred exposure to the credit union marketplace through NACUSO and supported advocacy to protect the regulatory climate for CUSO's. Vic had personal relationships with the people who ran these Platinum Partner CUSO's which helped immensely. Vic served as president from 2005 to 2007.

In 2007, Vic's duties at Member Gateways required him to give up the presidency. The next president also came from the NACUSO Board. Tom Davis served as president from 2007 to 2010. Tom has a doctorate in Industrial Psychology and was a former CEO of a CUSO in Colorado. Tom contributed a deeper understanding of the emotional component to collaboration and the personal disruption it can cause. People are uncomfortable with change for many reasons and that discomfort has an impact on the decision-making process. Tom's connections to the academic world resulted in a Collaboration Certificate Program at Pepperdine University's Business School. A class of a dozen credit union executives attended a week of lectures and after one year returned to campus to give their dissertation on a collaboration that they helped implement during the year. Unfortunately, the financial crisis hit and the demand for the Program diminished.

The fourth and current President is Jack Antonini. Jack is the first president who did not come from the Board. Jack has an impressive background. He was president of USAA Bank, one of the most admired customer-centric financial institutions in the world. He was also president of Cardtronics, the largest servicer of ATM's in the world. Jack is a member of one of MasterCard's Boards. He has broadened the reach of NACUSO beyond credit unions. NACUSO has benefited greatly from his credibility and leadership. Under Jack's leadership, an additional special membership level has been added to increase support, the Gold Level Membership with a $10,000 annual fee. Jack's connection to MasterCard has resulted in increased funding for speakers at NACUSO's Conferences. Recent past speakers include two sharks from Shark Tank and star athletes.

NACUSO has had eleven Board chairs, five of whom were credit union presidents (John Unangst, Ava Milosevich, Dennis Pierce, Mark Zook and Doug Petersen), four CUSO presidents (Norm Blahuta, Dan Balagna, Dave Serlo and Pete Snyder) and two consultants (Bob Dorsa and Tom Davis).

The story of NACUSO would not be complete without mentioning the staff. Shawna Luna, the Executive Assistant and Corporate Events Director, has been with NACUSO since 1996. She is the heart and soul of the organization. She worries about every detail. Members love her. Judy Sandberg served on the Board and was Interim COO from 2005 to 2007. She is a very savvy businessperson, having formed successful CUSO's. Bob Frizzle our CFO since 2005 is also the CFO at the CUSO CU Answers. NACUSO could not operate with Bob's advice. Denise Wymore is the super energetic Director of Membership and Advocacy Development. Denise has brought NACUSO into the world of social media and close member engagement.

The value proposition of NACUSO is three-fold: education, networking and advocacy. Conferences, webinars and articles provide the education and networking functions. Since 2013, the Conference has featured the Next Big Idea Competition, where innovators give their elevator speech on their new technology or service. The attendees vote on a winner. However, everyone wins. The attendees see a variety of new ideas and all the presenters get a valuable forum to pitch their ideas. The Conferenced is planned to make sure the attendees have adequate time to network. The Conference has multiple education tracks to ensure that information relevant to multiple types of CUSO's is provided. The six tracks are:

(a) investment services,
(b) insurance services,
(c) big data/data analytics,
(d) entrepreneur/CEO/business development,
(e) lending services, and
(f) innovation/operations/technology.

As the only dedicated CUSO trade association, NACUSO has always been very active in advocacy. A summary of the activity over the years is below:

In 1993, we met with Norm D'Amours, Chairman of NCUA, concerning loan participations. The rule at that time was that credit unions could only buy loan participation interests in loans at the time the loans were funded and not in closed loans. Chairman D'Amours agreed with our position that credit unions should be able to buy loan participation interests in closed loans as well. The NCUA loan participation regulation was amended as a result of our meeting. The change enabled credit unions to better mitigate credit risks, obtain liquidity, and increase lending capacity.

In 2002, I was asked by CUNA to serve on its committee to liaison with the Securities and Exchange Commission on the transition issues for credit union investment services programs caused by the adoption of the NCUA Incidental Powers Regulation and its effect on the SEC's Chubb No-Action Letter. The committee met with SEC representatives.

In 2007, NACUSO's advocacy helped prevent the issuance of Virginia state CUSO regulations that were more restrictive than NCUA's CUSO Regulations.

In 2008, NACUSO worked with NCUA to amend the CUSO Regulation to modernize the Regulation, including adding additional permitted services.

In 2009, NACUSO provided advice to the Washington Credit Union League on state CUSO regulatory changes and in 2014 the Washington State credit union regulator asked for NACUSO's comments on proposed state CUSO regulations.

In 2010, NCUA issued Letter 10-FCU-03 which applies to investment services disclosures. NACUSO's letter to NCUA resulted in a clarification letter by NCUA General Counsel.

In 2011, NACUSO commented on proposed changes to the Texas state CUSO regulations amendments that resulted in favorable changes to the final regulation.

In 2013, in a process that started in 2011, NCUA proposed an amendment to the CUSO Regulations requiring CUSO's to directly report to NCUA. NACUSO obtained the legal opinion of a prominent DC law firm on the issue of whether NCUA has the authority to require CUSO's to directly report to NCUA under the Federal Credit Union Act. While the law firm concluded that there were grounds to challenge NCUA's legal authority, there was not enough commitment from the NACUSO membership to fund a lawsuit as the reporting requirement was not so onerous as to justify the cost of litigation. No suit was brought.

In 2014, NCUA proposed to risk rate CUSO investments at 250 basis points. This would be a critical blow to the ability of credit unions to use CUSO's. NACUSO advocated hard for a reduction to 100 basis points and was successful.

In 2015, NCUA proposed extensive amendments to Member Business Lending Regulation. NACUSO worked the business lending CUSO's to advocate their positions on the proposed amendment. These efforts helped shape the business lending regulation we have today.

Also in 2015, Jack Antonini and I met with the staff of congressman and senators to oppose vendor authority. NACUSO joined with other trade associations to send a letter to Congress to prevent NCUA from obtaining vendor authority in an unrelated piece of legislation.

In 2017, NACUSO began advocating for NCUA to expand the CUSO powers to include the power to make all the types of loans a credit union can make.

NACUSO will continue to evolve and re-invent itself as the credit union and CUSO industry evolves. If you are interested in learning more about collaborations, particularly credit union collaborations, I urge you to become involved in NACUSO and attend the Annual Conference. www.nacuso.org. NACUSO is at the cross-roads of innovators and entrepreneurs both within and outside of credit unions. It is the place where credit unions can find collaborators that are prepared to plan and implement solutions. It is where collaborators meet and deals get down.

CHAPTER 7
PROFILES OF NOTABLE CUSO'S

One goal of this book is to preserve knowledge about significant CUSO's, specifically their services, history, impact on credit unions and the lessons learned. At this writing, I was able to collect information about four CUSO's: CU Answers, Financial Service Centers Cooperative, Ongoing Operations and Open Technology Solutions. I plan to add to these profiles in future editions or on the CUSO Guru Website as there are many other significant CUSO's with stories worth telling. In the meantime, I start with these four. I want to acknowledge the kind assistance of colleagues at the CUSO's who made sure that my information was accurate.

CU Answers – Randy Karnes, Bob Frizzle and Esteban Camargo

Financial Service Centers Cooperative – Sarah Canepa Bang and Bonnie Kramer

Ongoing Operations – Kirk Drake

Open Technology Solutions – Mike Atkins

CU ANSWERS, INC.

Services:	Core IT services technology and operational support services for credit unions
Ownership:	128 credit union owners
Clients:	182 credit unions
Formation:	1970
Location:	Grand Rapids, Michigan

Services

The original purpose of CU*Answers was to aggregate expertise and reduce costs of supporting third party core processing services. The CUSO developed its own core processing software called CU*Base. The services offered have evolved over time as new technologies have been introduced, but the mission to provide data processing services at a disruptive price remain both at CU*Answers and its affiliated organizations.

CU*Answers' affiliated CUSO, Xtend, provides the following services: bookkeeping, mortgage services, disaster recovery, business continuity, strategic planning, call center (both incoming and outgoing services), shared branching within the CU*Base network, forms exchange, member texting communications, conversion support, 5300 call report preparation and cooperative liquidity (through loan participations and certificates of deposit sales). Through AuditLink, Xtend formed a relationship with Trust Exchange to offer credit unions a comprehensive vendor management program.

CREDIT UNION COLLABORATIONS

While CU*Answers provides technical solutions in many of its services, there is equal emphasis on the relationship solutions; services that impact the relationship of the credit union to its members and the relationship between credit unions to enhance the ability of credit unions to serve members.

History and Structure

CU*Answers began as a service of Grand Rapids Teachers Credit Union. The credit union provided support to credit unions running a Fiserv core processing product. When Grand Rapids Teachers Credit Union requested capital to continue to provide the services, the credit union clients and Grand Rapids Teachers Credit Union decided to form a CUSO.

West Michigan Computer Co-Op, Inc. (WESCO) was organized as a non-stock cooperative to provide low-cost data processing service for credit unions. It initially had nine board members and approximately five staff members. All clients but one was on the Fiserv core IT platform. In 2003, WESCO changed its name to CU*Answers, to reflect that the CUSO was serving the broader credit union industry.

From the beginning, CU*Answers chose a cooperative model, one owner-one vote no matter what the size of the owner. The model is a carbon copy of the credit union model. Grand Rapids Teachers Credit Union saw the value in this model versus having unequal ownership rights based on the size of the owner or whether the owner was a founding owner.

Originally the CUSO was organized as a corporate non-stock entity with nine board members. In 1985, the

CUSO was reorganized as a corporate stock cooperative. All credit union owners have to be on the CU*Base platform. In 1990 the board of directors was reorganized to seven members comprised of the CEO's of credit union owners that have been owners for a minimum of one year. The directors are elected by the owners and serve three-year terms.

CU*Answers has also expanded its reach through investments in other organizations. In 2002, CU*Answers formed Xtend, Inc., a cooperative CUSO that provides a wide variety of services focusing on four main objectives: communication, collaboration, connection, and execution. The goal in creating a separate CUSO to provide these non-IT services was to broaden the clients served. Credit unions do not have to use CU*Base to participate as an owner or client of Xtend. Xtend invites all credit unions to avail themselves of the advantages of collaboration; i.e. market disruption through lower prices, access to new markets and the advantages of shared execution of common functions. Shared execution overcomes the problem that a credit union may have the tools but not the time to use them. Xtend is owned by 83 credit unions and CU*Answers.

While CU*Answers has a national footprint of clients, its Board challenged the management team of CU*Answers to walk its talk and engage in cooperative relationships with other CUSO's instead of engaging in a nationwide acquisition strategy. CU*Answers saw the advantages of working with CUSO's with a strong local commitment to their credit unions and affiliated with three organizations serving credit unions on the CU*Base platform: CU*South in Alabama, CU*Northwest in Washington State and Site-Four in South

Dakota. CU*Northwest and Site-Four are CUSO's that are co-owned by CU*Answers.

Both CU*Answers and CU*Northwest are winners of NACUSO's CUSO of the Year Award.

Credit Union Impact

CU*Answers has a unique investment and funding structure. There are four means of returning value to the owners. As all owners must use CU*Base, the first return is to have higher levels of expertise in IT support services at a lower cost than the credit unions could afford individually. The three other methods of returning value are actual payments made to the owners.

As a corporate cooperative in Michigan, CU*Answers pays a stock dividend and every owner gets the same amount (historically between 4% and 8% of the investment). This ensures all owners receive value just for being an owner and investing in CU*Answers. CU*Answers also pays a patronage dividend that correlates with the amount of direct business (revenue) done with the CUSO. The patronage dividend rewards the heavy users of CU*Answers' services. Note that CU*Answers does not discount fees to owners so volume discounts are recognized through patronage dividends. The final value return is through the use of debentures. If CU*Answers has a project that it wants to develop, it often issues debentures to finance the projects with interest returns that are slightly above market rates. This encourages an available stream of capital and provides another tangible benefit to the owners. The debentures are usually over-subscribed. CU*Answers often has to ration the debenture offering to be sure all those interested have an opportunity to participate.

As to the stock price, each year the board of directors establishes the purchase price for stock after considering the CPA audit. The investment amount for a new owner runs between 2% and 2 ½% of book value. The method of valuing the shares, encourages the owners to build the company and increase the equity and share value. CU*Answers has never had to re-capitalize in its 46 plus year history.

If an owner no longer is on CU*Base, it must leave CU*Answers. The owner is paid the book value of its shares. The stock cannot be sold by the owner other than back to CU*Answers.

Rather than organize as a limited liability company with pass through tax liability to the owners, CU Answers organized as a corporate cooperative and by doing so shielded the credit union owners from any income tax liability issues.

Lessons Learned

Ownership and alignment are the keys to success. The credit union owners decide the CUSO's priorities. If there are service issues, the owner/users solve them. CU*Answers is the tool of the credit union owners that collectively succeed by executing the credit unions' agenda and not an organization that provides useful services to credit unions. The difference sounds subtle but it is not. The long-term success of CUSO's depends upon a system that is implementing solutions to problems identified and driven by credit unions. If credit unions cease to see the

CUSO has their tool to solve their problems, the CUSO becomes just another vendor pushing a solution that may or may not be relevant to the credit unions.

CU Answers lives by the seven cooperative principals: (1) Voluntary and Open Membership; (2) Democratic Member Control; (3) Members' Economic Participation; (4) Autonomy and Independence; (5) Education, Training and Information; (6) Cooperation among Cooperatives; and (7) Concern for Community. CU*Answers has created video and educational pieces to promote the cooperative model. By aligning the CUSO structure with the credit union structure, conflict is reduced. CU*Answers believes that the cooperative model is powerful and should be celebrated. No one should feel like a cooperative is a second-class citizen to the for-profit world.

By working with other CUSO's, CU*Answers assembled a culture of mission aligned people with diverse opinions and talents. CU*Answers learned that aggregation of effort was very effective while the path of consolidating in one organization destroys the culture of the acquired organization without benefiting the member. Aggregation of CUSO's is aligning strengths and building a broader base and this is in line with the seven cooperative principles.

CU*Answers recognizes the concept of enlightened self-interest and works with it, not against it. People and credit unions want to be successful and unless the CUSO is helping them do that the CUSO will fail. Collaborations built only on feel good altruism will not work in the long run. The CUSO must demonstrate tangible financial and operational returns to the credit unions and the CUSO employees to be successful.

CU*Answers is more focused on creating an income statement than a balance sheet. It's a slow build, but so are credit unions.

The power of collaboration is the ability to create collaborative disruption through 1) pricing, 2) market access, or 3) shared execution.

If a credit union owns the solution, it will never be at odds with the strategic direction of the credit union. So, the build solution is favored over the buy solution.

FINANCIAL SERVICE CENTERS COOPERATIVE

Formation: July 23, 1990
Merger: Merged into COOP Financial Services on December 31, 2011.
Location: California
Services: Shared branching and ancillary services
Ownership: Originally 15 large California credit unions, now a part of COOP Financial Services
Clients: 330 credit unions at the time of the 2011 merger

The History

In December 1989, fifteen of the largest credit unions in California came together to build a branch network to compete with banks. FSCC was officially formed in July 1990. Bob Rose, the president of COOP Financial Services was the initial president of FSCC through a management agreement between the two companies. COOP was formed in 1981 to cooperatively run ATM networks.

The original plan included stand-alone shared branches. Four were built; in Lakewood (1991), Fountain Valley (1992), Concord (1992) and San Diego (1993). Due to the high costs of running the four branches, FSCC was not profitable. Bonne Kramer, a highly respected credit union technology expert, was hired in 1993 as its second CEO, to turn the company's fortunes around.

In 1994, FSCC decided to sell all four branches and transform the model into an outlet only model. In an outlet model, the credit unions designated a teller station within an existing credit union branch with intercept processing to connect to the shared branching network. This eliminated the huge stand-alone branch infrastructure costs and enabled FSCC to become self-sustaining.

In September 1998, FSCC expanded its client base from California and Nevada to include Oregon and Washington by acquiring a small shared branching network in Oregon and Washington named CU Access. The Board set its sights on a having a national presence. Realizing the amount of travel and relationship building a national sales effort would take. Bonnie recommended stepping into a COO position and hiring a new CEO. In July 1999, Sarah Canepa Bang became the third and last CEO of FSCC and Bonnie became its Chief Operating Officer. The concept of working remotely was a new concept in 1999. Sarah proved it worked. Sarah visited the offices in California regularly but her main office when she was not travelling was in her adopted home state of Washington.

In 2001, FSCC became an international shared branching network with locations on military bases in South Korea, Japan, Germany and Italy. The close personal and professional relationship between Sarah and Bonnie spurred the growth of FSCC through its merger with COOP in 2011.

The merger of FSCC into COOP was the final consolidation of the shared branching networks that began years earlier. In 1993, FSCC, Credit Union Service Corporation (CUSC) and COOP Network formed the Credit Union Service Centers Network, Inc. (CUSCNI) to facilitate transactions between networks. Service Center Corporation (SCC) joined in 1999. Until full consolidation occurred, CUSCNI operated as an umbrella organization to set rules and procedures to enable the networks to process transactions between the networks.

CUSC was formed in 1993 and headquartered in Atlanta. The owners were state leagues, CUNA and CUNA Mutual Group. There were 17 different state leagues with each state having its own network with separate rules and pricing. The state leagues served by CUSC followed the rules established by CUSC. Credit unions sat on the state league boards and some also sat on the CUSC board. CUSC started out with stand-alone branches but abandoned the model as too capital intensive. A 51% controlling interest in CUSC was purchased by COOP in 2007.

SCC was organized in 1974 as an ATM Network (SC24) with shared branching. SCC had a stand-alone branch network of 25 locations in Michigan in addition to outlets. In its stand-alone branches, each credit union had a dedicated teller station. There were small shared branching networks in Missouri, Wisconsin and the Washington DC area that had separate rules but used the SCC processing services. In May 2002, SCC was purchased by COOP for the ATM business. The shared branching services were incorporated into COOP Shared Branching, a subsidiary of COOP.

In 2011, FSCC was merged into COOP Shared Branching. The consolidation made sense for the credit union industry. Sarah continued with COOP as Chief Strategy Officer and then as Executive Vice-President of

Corporate Relations until her retirement in 2017. Bonnie retired in August 2016.

Business Structure

FSCC was originally formed as a for-profit corporation. In August 2000, FSCC converted to a cooperative corporation to permit patronage dividends to be returned to the owners based on usage. This encouraged and rewarded those owners that used the services of FSCC.

Investments and Funding

The original investing credit unions invested in FSCC and kept FSCC solvent until it could turn a profit. FSCC had its first profitable month in January 1996 after FSCC abandoned its stand-alone shared branching model and adopted a pure outlet model, thus reducing costs significantly. At the time of its merger into COOP, FSCC had capital of $17 million.

Benefits to the Credit Union

Shared branching enables credit union members to transact business in an exponentially larger branch network. A member who is travelling far from home can walk into a branch of a network member or up to a kiosk and can conduct most of the transaction the member could conduct in his or her home credit union branch. At the time of the merger, FSCC had 330 credit unions in its network, serving 40,121 members and executing 5.6 million transactions per month. The credit union members of the FSCC Network credit unions had the ability to access services at over 6,700 access points in all 50 states, Guam, Puerto Rico, Italy, Germany and the United Kingdom. The service access points included a monumental deal with Southland to place kiosks in 7-11 stores. The unique cooperative nature of credit unions enables this network to exist and prosper.

At the time of the merger with COOP, FSCC provide the following additional services on its own or in collaboration with other providers (some of which are CUSO's): virtual kiosks, currency exchange, savings software, mobile banking, call centers, remote capture and business continuity services.

<u>People</u>
Bonnie Kramer started her career with credit unions in DeKalb, Illinois. She started out as a volunteer of this newly formed municipal credit union in 1968 when she worked in the City of DeKalb accounting department (she was good with numbers). There were other small credit unions in and around DeKalb. Bonnie became a self-taught technologist and persuaded seven credit unions to consolidate their core processing services around the CUNA Data Platform which she managed in the DeKalb Credit Union Service Center. The credit unions she managed contracted with the Service Center for all services. Bonnie worked Monday through Saturday at the DeKalb Credit Union Service Center with Wednesday's off to serve the members of these credit unions. On Saturday mornings, she would have coffee and donuts for the members to show her appreciation for being credit union members.

CUNA Data was supported by EDS. In 1981, EDS bought CUNA Data. Recognizing the need for credit union industry people to sell and integrate the product, EDS offered

Bonnie a job. Bonnie moved to Texas. A new field division was being tested in the West and she was transferred to California on a temporary job assignment for serving credit unions locally in the Western region. Since the EDS office was located in the California Credit Union League, a job opened up at COOP in 1986 in sales. She was EVP until she took the job at FSCC first as CEO then as COO. When COOP Shared Branching acquired FSCC, Bonnie became VP of Business Development and Operations until her retirement in 2017. Sarah cannot say enough about the contributions that Bonnie made to FSCC. If there was any way possible to find a process or technological solution to a credit union need, Bonnie would deliver it.

As for Sarah, she is an Herb Wagner Individual Achievement Award Winner for a reason. She is from Baraboo Wisconsin, went to the University of Wisconsin and during college worked for Elroy "Crazy Legs" Hirsch, Director of Athletics. She worked for the Oregon Credit Union League. Sarah is famous for having the most flamboyant collection of shoes in the industry. However, it does not take long when you are around her to appreciate her business sense and people skills. Her enthusiastic support of credit unions and credit union causes like the Children's Charitable Network is genuine and contagious. Just as Bonnie, Sarah was the right person at the right time to grow FSCC into the success it became.

Sarah lists notable board members of FSCC which includes: Stan Hollen, CEO of The Golden 1 Credit Union; Carl Stewart, CEO of Water & Power Credit Union; Steve Dahlstrom, CEO of Spokane Teachers Credit Union; Steve

Stapp, CEO of San Francisco Federal Credit Union; Judy McCartney, CEO of Orange County's Credit Union; Tom Graham, CEO of Kinecta Credit Union; Pat Smith, CEO of Unitus Credit Union; Ted Dennis, CEO of Point Loma Credit Union; Roger Michaels, CEO of IQ Credit Union; Tom Stewart, CEO of Western Credit Union; Larry Sharp, CEO of Arrowhead Credit Union; and Ed Callahan, CEO of Patelco Credit Union followed by Andy Hunter.

Lessons Learned

A transaction-based business needs to reward those participants that generate the fees through patronage. The cooperative model works best for this type of service.

Transaction fees alone cannot support a branch. FSCC was not making any interest or other non-interest income. A stand-alone model will not work. A stand-alone model with dedicated tellers for each credit union is impossible to support.

The advantages of a fully integrated national network with common rules overcome any desire to customize your own network and rules. Satisfying egos is not worth the price.

CREDIT UNION COLLABORATIONS

ONGOING OPERATIONS, LLC

Services:	Business Continuity Planning, Hosted Cloud Solutions, Information Security, Disaster Recovery, Telecom Services
Ownership:	18 credit unions, 3 CUSO's and 5 senior management employees
Clients:	160 Credit Unions, 15 CUSO's and 35 Others
Formation:	2005
Location:	Hagerstown, Maryland

Services

Ongoing Operations ("OGO") started out providing business continuity services with off-site work sites within driving distance of major metropolitan areas. OGO later purchased a cloud service provider to offer hosted cloud solutions. OGO also provides information security, disaster recovery and telecom solutions. OGO has 45 employees located in 12 states.

History and Structure

In 2001, just a week after 9/11, there was an anthrax attack on government offices in Washington DC. Anthrax powder was being sent by mail to government offices and most government offices were closed to clean up the powder and to prevent further incidents until the attack could be stopped. For those credit unions located in government offices, that meant they shut down operations and had difficulty continuing to serve members.

In response, several credit unions decided they needed a dependable business continuity solution. The

CREDIT UNION COLLABORATIONS

existing business continuity services vendors promised a site to run a credit union if there was a business continuity issue but did not guarantee that the credit union client would have a space if the problem was wide-spread and other clients also needed the space. Credit unions wanted dedicated space that they could count on at a desired location with favorable pricing. That need and desire led several DC area credit unions, mostly government sponsored, to form OGO.

Judy Sandberg, a CUSO professional and consultant, met with the credit unions in the pre-formation process and encouraged the group to form a CUSO. Two of the key CEO's to form OGO were Lindsay Alexander of NIH Federal Credit Union and Juri Valdov of Northwest Federal Credit Union. The original investors were NIH Federal Credit Union, Northwest Federal Credit Union, Transportation Federal Credit Union, Department of Labor Federal Credit Union, Synergy One Federal Credit Union, HEW Federal Credit Union, Agriculture Federal Credit Union, Quorum Federal Credit Union, Fort Belvoir Federal Credit Union and PSCU. Most of the credit unions were DC area government sponsored credit unions. Lindsay had a young CIO named Kirk Drake who saw the vision and was willing to jump into this new concept. Kirk became CEO of OGO. Lindsay was the first Board Chair, followed by Juri. Bruno Sementilli of Quorum Federal Credit Union succeeded Juri as Chair and was Chair during the re-capitalization process. Steve Salzer, General Counsel of PSCU succeeded Bruno as Chair.

OGO's first business continuity site was Hagerstown, Maryland. Hagerstown is about fifty miles west of the

Washington DC metro area which is close enough to drive to in a short period of time but out of the power grid and immediate area in case of a disaster in the DC metro area. OGO has had other recovery sites in Oregon, Colorado and Arizona (co-located at PSCU's data facility). The Oregon site has since been closed.

OGO was the first CUSO to enter the business continuity space primarily dedicated to credit unions. There was an early decision by management and the board to revise OGO from a cost containment strategy to an aggressive strategy to obtain market share before other competitors entered the space.

Initially, OGO served credit unions and non-credit unions. The technology business is expensive and cash flow was needed and the income from the non-credit union business helped cash flow in the early stages of OGO.

OGO bought Cloudworks, Inc. in 2011. Cloudworks provided hosted cloud computing services. Kirk saw that the future of computing services for credit unions was going to be cloud-based. That meant that the traditional business continuity market was going to be altered and reduced in importance. If you can run a cloud-based system, you will not need as much infrastructure for business continuity. Hosted cloud-based services also opened a number of other service opportunities. Telecom services were added.

OGO's ownership expanded not only with additional credit unions but also with other large CUSO's. COOP Financial Services and FSCC became investors. OGO's management also became co-owners which is typical for an IT company.

OGO is a limited liability company. Class A owners are credit unions and all others are Class B. There is no difference in rights except that there must be at least one Class A and one Class B representative on the Board of Managers. The Managers are elected for three-year terms on a rotating basis.

Each of the original owners invested $150,000 to begin operations. The debt service from the Cloudworks purchase, the constant need to re-invest in technology, owner service fee discounts and a slower credit union adoption rate for cloud services than anticipated, required the owners to recapitalize OGO in 2015.

Credit Union Impact
Initially, OGO was formed to provide better services at a lower cost. That was successful. OGO owners were able to have guaranteed seats to operate their credit unions in the event of a disaster at a cost which was lower than charged by third party providers. There was a decision, perhaps implicitly, to revise OGO into a for-profit venture, to capture market share and expand into other services. While the credit unions as clients continued to benefit from this expansion, OGO's rapid expansion of services placed the capital situation under stress.

Lessons Learned
The biggest lesson is that technology services require a great deal of capital and a source of capital on a regular

basis. Credit unions are conservative in nature and are comfortable with making an initial capital investment but are not willing to be a source of continuing investments. This is especially so when the CUSO is ahead of the industry adoption curve and the revenue is delayed.

Cash flow is king in any business. It was great to give owners discounts but not at the price of insufficient cash flow. Owner discounts have been discontinued.

Be intentional on the nature of the business. Some owners did not understand the change in strategy, moving from cost containment to a for-profit venture. That created problems with some owners that did not understand or agree to the change.

Be aware of the effect of unit sales on owner capital. As new owners were brought on the price of units has both risen and declined. This price change can affect the valuation of the units held by existing owners.

Do not underestimate the importance of skin in the game for management. OGO is one of the few CUSO's that permits management to have an ownership interest. Senior management has invested their own money in OGO which is a signal to existing and potential investors that management believes in OGO's future and will work hard to keep OGO successful.

Also, do not underestimate the people aspect of collaboration. You have to work with people that understand the benefits of collaboration and that it is a "long game.". People who "get it" appreciate the advantages of collectively controlling key services and are willing to work for the common goals without imposing operational conditions that would lessen the value of the collaboration. There were times when owners and potential owners, raised objections that would impede the CUSO's functionality or capital position. When faced with that opposition, a CUSO Board is faced with the decision of accommodating individual desires or inviting the person with the objection to "step away from the table" and withdraw from the collaboration if they are unhappy with it. If your goal is to have an efficient and effective collaboration, you cannot have a dozen different ways of accommodating one-off requests.

The owner dissatisfaction can come from (a) a change in the credit union owner's management or board who no longer see the advantages of the collaboration, (b) a change in the strategic direction of the CUSO, (c) the loss of confidence in the CUSO to achieve the agreed goals, or (d) a CUSO's adverse financial impact upon the credit union owner. If some owners want to disassociate, it is in the best interest to work out terms to accommodate the request if possible. All the people in the boat need to be rowing in the same direction.

Personal contacts can make all the difference as they do in the rest of the business world. For example, Juri Valdov was able to interest COOP Financial Services to become an investor through his relationship with Stan Hollen. The decision by COOP was made after its due diligence but the ability to connect personally with potential investors and clients is a significant advantage. If your credibility precedes you, doors open more quickly.

OPEN TECHNOLOGY SOLUTIONS, LLC

Formation:	2003
Location:	Denver Colorado
Services:	IT Support for Third Party Software
Ownership:	3 credit union owners
Clients:	3 credit union owners

The History

Bellco Credit Union converted to the Open Solutions, Inc., ("OSI") core IT platform in 2001. Bellco found that it was spending a lot of money in adapting and integrating OSI into the Credit Union's operations. Doug Ferraro, the CEO of Bellco, and Mike Atkins, the CIO, concluded, over fine wine and cocktail napkins, that they needed to build a better business model, one with multiple credit unions providing the IT support on an aggregated basis to reduce cost, increase efficiencies and hire the highest level of talent.

As it happened, Bethpage Federal Credit Union and State Employees Federal Credit Union of New York ("SEFCU") were both considering the OSI platform. Both were being advised by the Tower Group and both visited Bellco. Tower advised them not to take on the conversion to OSI on their own due to the costs and complications. SEFCU decided to go with another core but Bethpage and Bellco began discussions. Doug Ferraro and Kirk Kordeleski, CEO of Bethpage, began to talk about the business model, which resulted in the formation of Open Technology Solutions, LLC ("OTS") on June 21, 2003.

In 2005, First Tech Credit Union came on board and went live in 2006. Tragically, Mike Osborne, the EVP and CFO of First Tech and the champion of joining OTS, died suddenly a week after the First Tech went live.

State Employees Credit Union of Maryland was added as a member in 2007. There were four owners/users until 2011 when First Tech withdrew.

The four CEO's who made the decision to collaborate on such a key service deserve a mention as it is a big decision to make: Doug Ferraro (Bellco), Kirk Kordeleski (Bethpage), Tom Sargent (First Tech) and Ron Staatz (SECU).

First Tech merged with Addison Avenue Federal Credit Union in 2010. First Tech, which has Nike and Microsoft in its field of membership, had multiple requests to customize the IT services to meet the particular needs of their members. Customization was an added cost to the requesting credit union. The added costs, the increased scale of First Tech from the merger and new leadership not committed to the collaborative model, contributed to the reasons for the withdrawal of First Tech.

Open Solutions, Inc. was purchased by Fiserv in 2013. The OSI Platform was renamed DNA by Fiserv.

Business Structure
OTS is a limited liability company. The three-owner credit union CEO's constitute the Board of Managers plus

the Chief Operating Officer, Mike Atkins. Open Solutions, LLC (now Fiserv) has a nominal ownership interest but no management powers. The CUSO business model was new to OSI and they wanted to participate to see how this experiment developed.

The OTS office is in Denver near Bellco. Each credit union has local IT support staff. In the case of Bethpage and SECU, they have retained a Chief Information Officer. The local IT staff is in charge of internal networking functions while OTS handles the overall network function.

The Manager meetings are monthly with most being by telephone. All decisions have been unanimous. The COO attends each credit union's board planning session each year to ensure that there is alignment on key strategic issues.

Investments and Funding
Each credit union has invested the same amount of money in OTS and each credit union pays the same for the services provided. If a credit union wants to have a customized service unique to them, there is an upcharge for that service. If another credit union later uses that service, there is a cost sharing adjustment.

Even though one owner is substantially larger than the other two, there has not been a change in the equal price per member. They have talked about charging on a tier basis but given the ease of scaling technology services, they have not pursued that plan.

Employees

OTS has approximately 160 employees, most working out of Denver but some employees are off-site.

Products and Services

The primary service OTS provides is to be provide the in-house support for the third-party core technology services and the acquisition and integration of other software services. OTS is the collective back office for the three credit unions to advise and implement software solutions. OTS manages the network that provides the services to the credit unions. OTS does the due diligence on IT providers and implements cyber-security tools. OTS is a Co-Sourced CUSO for technology support services.

Benefits to the Credit Union

The three current owners are very large credit unions. In 2019, Bellco has $4.7 billion in assets and 336,228 members, Bethpage has $8.9 billion in assets and 400,005 members, and SECU has $3.8 billion in assets and 257,587 members. All three credit unions are capable of hiring expertise to run their IT solutions but they all recognized that they could perform those services much better in a collaboration. They are big credit unions but are modestly sized financial institutions in the greater universe, the one in which all credit unions have to compete.

The CUSO aims to provide a better level of service, a higher level of expertise, fast to market execution and all at a lower cost per credit union. The goal was to take the service levels of each of the credit unions and meet or exceed the highest standard of the three. OTS has delivered. The up time is 99.98%. OTS was down only 50 minutes in a year.

The satisfaction level on the service tickets is over 97%. OTS is a best of class IT service provider.

Mike Atkins estimates that each credit union owner saves around $2 million per year based on reduced staffing needs. He also estimates that each credit union owner saves another $2 million per year based on the collective increased bargaining power. When you have combined assets of $11.8 billion and 753,000 members you have extraordinary bargaining power.

The positive experience of this CUSO encouraged the formation of Shared Services Solutions ("S3") to provide a host of back office services which are made much more feasible by being on the same IT Platform that is collectively managed.

Lessons Learned

In hindsight there were a lot of obstacles that could have been avoided if there was one integrated system instead of each credit union maintaining its own separate internal IT staff, CIO's and security at the desk top level. The differences in the chart of accounts made apples to apples comparisons difficult. Credit unions measured services and expenses differently. Each credit union had its own agreement with the core provider.

Although very successful, OTS could have enjoyed more success more quickly if the owners turned over the entire IT operations to OTS with a standardized chart of accounts. Easy to say but that would have been a very difficult decision for the credit unions. Note that credit union agreements with the core and other software providers should have a co-terminus provision so that OTS and the credit unions can move as one if there are changes in the providers. Another way to manage the co-terminus issue is for the agreements to be with OTS with the right of OTS to serve the credit unions.

Each credit union had their own preferred software providers for the various services but over time the credit unions worked through that issue and landed on single providers. They did this with the philosophy that each service most likely has three top providers who might have different bells and whistles in their products but each could serve the needs of the credit unions. The CEO's give their staff the ability to make selections but if they cannot then the CEO's will come in and make the decision immediately. If the staff wants to be part of the decision, they need to reach a consensus among them. The technique has worked and very few decisions have to be "kicked upstairs" to the CEO's.

It is critical that the CEO's have a high level of personal trust among them. They tell their staff to look first to the partner credit unions to find an existing solution they can use or develop a collaborative solution. The CEO's have worked hard to "institutionalize" the collaboration with the buy-in of the credit union boards and staff so that when there is a CEO change, a compatible CEO will be found to support the collaboration.

CREDIT UNION COLLABORATIONS

EPILOGUE

I hope this book has given you insight on how credit union collaborations are conceived, structured and operated. Additional information on credit union collaborations and CUSO's can be found in Brian Lauer's book *CUSOs* (available on Amazon), on the NACUSO website (www.nacuso.org), the Messick Lauer & Smith website (www.cusolaaw.com) and my CUSO Guru website (www.cuso.guru). Yes, that is a real domain. I encourage you to collect information, network with colleagues and become active in NACUSO. If you want to fish, go where the fish are. The credit union collaboration fish are at NACUSO.

The collaborations lessons learned in the credit union world are lessons about how people learn a new way of managing the business challenges facing them. It comes easier to some than for others. The good news is that there are success stories to affirm that building a collaboration is worth the effort. The lessons learned by credit unions can be applied to other organizations, especially other cooperatives and fraternal organizations.

Finding a good collaboration partner is like finding a good travel friend. You have lots of friends but how many friends are good travel buddies? Travel friends will be on time, keep their promises, pay their fair share, be flexible when things do not go as planned, and have a can-do attitude. Find your travel friends in the credit union world and find ways to leverage the power of collaboration.

Someday every credit union will use collaborations extensively...because those will be the credit unions that survive to serve their members.

Guy A. Messick
November 21, 2019

APPENDIX

SAMPLE COLLABORATION POLICY

A. Background and Purpose

Collaborations are an essential element in the operations of the Credit Union. Collaborations enable the Credit Union to be able to provide services more efficiently and cost effectively and to provide valuable financial services to members that cannot be offered through the traditional credit union model. The purpose of the Collaboration Policy is to provide guidance to the Credit Union in considering, selecting, implementing, monitoring and managing collaborations in order to enhance the success of the collaborations and the benefits to the credit union. Most collaborations will be through co-ownership of a credit union service organization ("CUSO").

B. Definitions

    1. Collaboration Manager: A senior staff position who reports directly to the President and works with the staff and board to help identify, select, implement,

CREDIT UNION COLLABORATIONS

   monitor and manage the Credit Union's collaboration relationships under this Collaboration Policy.
2. Collaboration Partner: A party with whom there is a co-ownership of a CUSO. The Collaborative Partner may or may not be a credit union or CUSO.
3. Subject Matter Expert. The Credit Union staff that is knowledgeable about the subject matter of the collaboration in question and works with the Collaboration Manager in identifying, selecting, implementing, monitoring and managing the specific subject matter of the collaboration; e.g., mortgage lending, collections, IT support.
4. Service Provider: A third party service provider which may or may not be a CUSO.

C. Goals of Collaborations

Identify the goals of a collaboration which may include one or more of the following:

1. Production of non-interest income;
2. Acquiring more loans and interest income;
3. Expanding financial services to members;
4. Lowering or containing operational costs;
5. Lowering or containing vendor costs;
6. Increasing efficiencies and timeliness of services;
7. Attracting and retaining experienced and talented staff; and
8. Creating an entrepreneurial culture to foster innovation and growth opportunities.

D. Parameters for the Selection of Collaborations

1. In selecting Collaboration Partners, the Credit Union shall consider the following factors:

a. Does the Collaboration Partner have goals compatible with the Credit Union's goals?
b. Does the Collaboration Partner have a compatible risk tolerance for the business risks associated with a collaboration?
c. Does the Collaboration Partner have successful experiences with other collaborations?
d. Do the Credit Union staff and board have a good working relationship with the Collaboration Partner?
e. Does the Collaboration Partner have the financial ability to meet its commitments of the collaboration?
f. Does the Collaboration Partner have the full support of its board and staff to meet its commitments?
g. Does the Collaboration Partner have the ability to make timely decisions?
h. Do you trust the Collaboration Partner to timely meet its commitments?
i. Does the Collaboration Partner have an entrepreneurial culture?
j. Is the Collaboration Partner open to new solutions to achieve its goals?
k. Does the Collaboration Partner have the same sense of urgency to implement the collaboration?

2. If there are preferences with regard to the geographic location, size or other characteristics for a Collaboration Partner in a particular collaboration, these should be identified.

3. The CUSO should be structured in a manner consistent with its goals which include attention to ownership, profit and loss and management issues.

Unless there are compelling interests to justify a variance (and there often can be), the agreements should have the following characteristics:

   a. The Credit Union shall have management control over the CUSO at least commensurate with its relative capital contribution.
   b. Profit and loss should be shared commensurate with the Credit Union's relative capital contribution and/or patronage component (percentage of revenue brought to the CUSO).
   c. Tax issues and flexibility of structure should be considered in selecting the type of CUSO entity.
   d. There should be clear procedures and financial terms for Collaboration Partners desiring to enter and exit the CUSO.
   e. All Collaboration Partners shall be users of the services of the collaboration and there shall be procedures for Collaboration Partners to be compelled to leave the collaboration if they are not fully supporting the efforts of the collaboration.
   f. Minimum service levels should be stated with the right to terminate the services agreement if not met after a right to cure.

5. The Board shall approve all collaborations in which the Credit Union makes an investment.

E. Administration of Collaboration Policy

The CEO shall appoint a Collaboration Manager. The duties of the Collaboration Manager shall be to implement the Collaboration Policy. The Collaboration Manager will work with the Subject Matter Expert as may be designated for a specific collaboration. The Collaboration Manager's duties include:

1. Identification of Collaborative Opportunities
   a. Acquiring knowledge of collaboration opportunities through research and networking.
   b. Bringing to the attention of the senior staff collaboration opportunities, especially those collaborations that will enhance and promote the strategic goals of the Credit Union.

2. Evaluating a Collaboration Opportunity
   a. Identify the goals of a collaboration opportunity and the ability of the collaboration opportunity to achieve those goals.
   b. Consider the need for the collaboration to overcome a challenge versus the cost in time and capital to join or create a specific collaboration.
   c. Identify regulatory issues to consider.
   d. Identify operational risks associated with the collaboration.
   e. Identify the business risks in joining or creating a collaboration versus not joining or creating a collaborative solution.
   f. Consider the method and cost to disassociate from a collaboration if it is not successful.
   g. Support the staff and the board in the planning process as strategy and service solutions are considered.

3. Selection of Collaborative Partners and Service Providers
   a. Working with Credit Union management and the Subject Matter Expert to establish the criteria for the selection of a specific collaboration solution.
   b. Administering the selection process.

CREDIT UNION COLLABORATIONS

    c. Coordinating the due diligence on potential Collaboration Partners and the collaboration.
    d. Acting as liaison between the Credit Union and potential Collaboration Partners.
    e. Presentation of results to staff and/or board.

4. Implementation of Collaborations
    a. Negotiation of agreements with Collaboration Partners consistent with the Collaboration Policy and the needs identified by the Subject Matter Expert.
    b. Coordinating the integration of the collaboration with the Credit Union, including the education of the Credit Union's staff on the purpose and value of the collaboration.
    c. Reviewing and recommending to the CEO the performance incentives to the Credit Union staff, as may be applicable, to incent them to support the success of the collaboration.
    d. Coordinating the resolution of any implementation and operational issues between the Credit Union staff and the Collaboration Partner staff.

5. Monitoring Collaborations
    a. Collecting performance reports from the Collaboration Partner and conducting review sessions with them on no less than a quarterly basis.
    b. Providing the performance reports to the Credit Union senior staff and board.

6. Managing Collaborations
    a. Marking recommendations to the CEO regarding actions to improve the collaboration.
    b. Counseling the Credit Union staff and the Collaboration Partner on remedial actions to

CREDIT UNION COLLABORATIONS

address service issues and, if not satisfactorily resolved, recommend to the CEO in writing actions to hold persons or organizations accountable.

c. Coordinating the implementation of procedures to manage the operational and regulatory risks.

d. Interaction with the regulators and the Credit Union's retained professionals regarding collaborations.

e. Coordinating the termination and transition of collaborations.

This Policy is illustrative and not meant to be used without legal review for the specific client situation.

CREDIT UNION COLLABORATIONS

ABOUT THE AUTHOR

Guy A. Mesick is an attorney with over thirty years of experience helping credit unions plan, organize and implement collaborations through credit union service organizations ("CUSO's"). He has counselled credit unions in every state and given presentations at over 100 meetings and conferences. His professional experience includes the following:

- General Counsel to the National Association of Credit Union Service Organizations and NACUSO's Regulatory Advocate 1987 – 2020.
- Founding partner in the law firm of Messick Lauer & Smith 1988 – 2020.
- Honored as one of the initial three CUSO Pioneers in America's Credit Union Museum in Manchester, NH.
- Guest presenter on collaboration at the University of Cork, Ireland and Pepperdine University, California.
- Author of *Credit Union Collaborations – Lessons Learned* and *The Guide for Credit Unions Providing Investment and Insurance Services*.
- Former Co-Chair of the American Bar Association's Credit Union Governance Sub-Committee.

Guy lives in Media, Pennsylvania and Sarasota, Florida with his wife Lucy. They have five children and five grandchildren.

Although Guy will be retired from providing legal services effective January 1, 2021, Guy plans to continue to consult with credit unions and other cooperative organizations on how to create successful collaborations. He maintains a website called the CUSO Guru with articles and presentations, www.cuso.guru.

CREDIT UNION COLLABORATIONS

Made in the USA
Lexington, KY
23 November 2019